HATHAWAY

Autobiography

To: A viery dear person interested
Ms. Martha M. Abdelsalam -

Enjoy & thanks.
Love
Prudence
Sept '04

HATHAWAY

by

Prudence Burns Burrell

HARLO DETROIT

ISBN 0-8187-0307-5

Printed by Harlo Press, 50 Victor, Detroit, Michigan 48203

HATHAWAY

The rampant Mississippi River may have caused destruction and chaos in this small village-like town of Southern Illinois, but it did not interrupt the regularly scheduled gossip at the end of Elm Street. A newspaper could never survive the juicy gossip transported as the "gospel truth" from the mouths of predominately "Hard Shell" Baptist people who gather at these sessions which took the place of newspapers. Come Hell or high water, a couple of men decided they would not let the overflow and flooding of the Mississippi curtail their session. During the night an incident had occurred and they were not about to let those fleeing the flood waters leave without this choice piece of gossip. Liz, the night prowler, who went up and down alleys peering into the "shot gun" houses' back doors or windows had witnessed this incident and, like Paul Revere, spread the word.

"Man, I told you that Elizabeth gal was pregnant again."

"No! You said she was just getting fat!"

"Fat hell! Last night, one hour past 12 midnight, she gave birth to another bastard. This time it's a girl. She was born on March 23rd. They have already named her "Hathaway." Ever heard of such name for a girl? I bet that Waters boy is the father. Poor Maggie has another bastard to feed. You know they wouldn't take that Waters boy into the Army, and I saw him in and out of that house a lot especially when her mama, Maggie, left for work everyday."

Maggie was the head cook at the "Veneloy" Central Illinois Train Station. She was an excellent cook and handled those huge cooking utensils like a man. After work she'd stop by the only bar in town for a small bucket of draft beer to take home along with shrimp she had taken from the restaurant. Tired and weary from work and overweight Maggie would trudge home, flop down, drink and share the goodies she had picked up along the way.

Maggie, after having been freed from slavery in Kentucky, married and migrated to this little Southern Illinois town while her mother, two brothers and one sister went to a Northern Illinois town. Also, the job as head cook was another factor that helped her to make up her mind to settle in this town. Money and jobs were scarce. Her husband did not have a steady job and with two children to feed, she felt she was lucky.

Maggie also felt that to be free of her domineering mother was just as exciting as when the shackles of slavery were removed.

This little southern Illinois town is very unique, yet not too different from other small towns. A cast system made it unique. Whites lived in one section with only a street as a divider from the blacks. The black section had divisions according to wealth. Middle incomes lived in fairly nice homes with inside toilets. Most of the men either worked on the railroads, as farmers, or a collectors for the numbers racket. One family was in the real estate business. At one time this little town had the highest Central Railroad payroll in the country.

Poorer people, including Hathaway's family, lived in predominately "shot gun" houses with either wooden or outside flush toilets. Electricity was not in every home. How Hathaway hated cleaning the globes from the lamps that burned kerosene!

This town had the most hypocritical people in the world. Some of the elite women were society prostitutes. One of the prostitutes led the church choir down the aisle every Sunday with "Onward Christian Soldiers." Some women would shout and knock over benches, stating they felt the spirit. The Deacons would run over to hold them. After church, Hathaway would run through the alleys and observe the deacon, who did most of the holding at church, slip into the back door of the shouting woman. Hathaway thought to herself - the shouting was an act to make a date and meet "Thank God, he asked me."

As dawn came, Maggie, half asleep and tired from the ordeal of Elizabeth giving birth to Hathaway, reflected over her life. Her husband had died and left her a widow with two children to support. She had managed fairly well through the years. Her son died from small pox and Elizabeth had overcome her attack. Now she is having babies one after another in spite of her constant pleading for Elizabeth to finish school. She gave her everything money could possibly buy: beautiful clothes which brought out her beauty and charmed the boys. They all wanted to date Elizabeth. Why couldn't she see and know their intentions? Regardless of the situation, she was elated over her beautiful granddaughter. Perhaps Hathaway would bring joy and pride to the family. From the way she made her entrance into the world, she had already begun to make many demands; a true Aries!

Maggie wished her own mother, Mollie, could see Hathaway. She would have loved her great-granddaughter - maybe some of Mollie's hatred toward granddaughter Elizabeth would melt. Mollie had constantly begged Maggie to move up to the Northern Illinois town where she could have the support and guidance of her brothers, sister and mother. Maggie did not want this because her mother had voiced her opinion many times; accused her of not knowing how to handle her daughter, Elizabeth, and that she was working herself to death caring for a wayward daughter and her bastards. Maggie's two brothers worked for Illinois Central Railroad; one brother married and his wife died a year later. The other brother was married and divorced with two sons from the marriage. The two sons, one named Leland, the younger, and the other named Willie. Leland moved to Detroit and Willie lived with his grandmother, Mollie. Mollie worshipped him and felt he could do no evil. Mollie continued to dominate their lives - as a doting old widow. When she was freed from slavery her master gave her everything for her home in Illinois - crystal, linens, furniture, horse and buggy, even lap rugs when riding in the buggy. She had been taught to read and write. With what her master had given along with hard work, Mollie had made tremendous progress. She was classified as the well-to-do grand matron of this Northern Illinois town. She even had a telephone, which was very rare in the twenties. The home was a beautiful duplex with Mollie on one side and roomers in the other side. No! Maggie would not uproot her family and once again become dominated by her mother. She could manage on her own, come hell or high water.

Maggie's elations were replaced with another sad thought - Elizabeth had married Barnes before Hathaway was born but she knew, and so did the gossiping people of the town know that her Elizabeth was pregnant before the marriage. Barnes knew also but confessed that his love for Elizabeth overshadowed everything else in his life - that he wanted to make her happy. He had recently returned from the war and stated he was ready to settle and get his life together. Maggie welcomed him into the household. Since her husband had died, she felt a man about the house would help to make a good family relationship once more. She hoped it would work out, at least her daughter was now married. Perhaps Mollie would be happy and Maggie hoped her mother would develop a better relationship with the family.

Maggie's household began to settle into a regular routine with her as the dominant figure. Barnes was not allowed to become head of the family. No one was to discipline Hathaway. She was her granddaughter and she was to grow up to be a fine young lady. As Hathaway began to grow, she knew she could twist her grandmother around every finger. She began talking at an early age but was slow to walk. This worried Maggie. She had used all of the old folks wive's tales; even bathed her legs in dish water to strengthen the muscles. As Maggie cuddled Hathaway, she prayed that her granddaughter would not be an invalid. However, Hathaway talked, demanded and ordered people around; why couldn't she walk? One day, Harris, a close fried of the family, came to visit. Maggie began to cry and told him how worried she was about Hathaway not walking. She would soon be two years old. Harris told Maggie that she had spoiled Hathaway, catered to her every whim. He assured Maggie that he would make Hathaway walk and asked that she fetch a bottle of red pop. When Hathaway saw the red stuff, she began to giggle, point and beg for it. Harris insisted that if she walked to him he would give her the red stuff. Hathaway began a tantrum, screaming and demanding with the same tactics she used on her grandmother who would say, "Okay, baby!" And give in to her. Harris was determined. Finally Hathaway realized that this was not her grandmother and, if she was to have the red stuff, she had to get up and walk. This she did! Was Maggie ever happy! She jumped up and down screaming that her baby could walk! From that day on Hathaway could no longer pretend. Later, Hathaway learned that RED POP had blown her bag. Hathaway called her grandmother Maggie, "Mama," and her mother, Elizabeth, was called "Mauyea."

Barnes began to resent the threat to his masculinity; he was only a figure head. He and Elizabeth began to quarrel frequently. Hathaway would eavesdrop on the quarrels, not that it was too difficult to hear; after all, just so much privacy could be had in a "shot gun" four room house. While these arguments were in session, Hathaway would get into mischief, fighting with the neighbors' children, her smaller brothers, running the hen with her little chicks under the house, or beating the family dog which she hated. When Elizabeth would attempt to punish Hathaway, she would run to the restaurant where Mama Maggie worked and jump into her lap for security and protection. Hathaway would sit on the step just outside the kitchen door where she could keep an eye on her grandmother. At the end of the day they would walk hand in hand to the bar for beer, then home to drink and eat the little red things called shrimp.

Hathaway knew when she had been extremely bad. As she sat on the steps waiting for her grandmother, her actions bugged her as they ran through her mind. Why couldn't she be a good little girl? Here her grandmother worked hard so that she could have everything nice: beautiful fancy dresses with long sashes of ribbon for every dress. Hathaway would just as soon snatch the ribbon from her hair and either give it away or throw it away. Once she gave her little brother a bottle of turpentine to drink. He kept saying, "Give me some." She turned up the bottle and said, “Here, drink it all!” The doctors had to pump his stomach. Once she became so angry she knocked another brother unconscious against the corner bricks that held up the house. Unaware that the little girl next door and she had identical Easter outfits, and due to the fact that Hathaway’s outfit was taken away when she gave the turpentine to her brother which caused the unconscious episode, as a punishment she was told that the Easter outfit had been given away.

Easter Sunday, Ellen, the little girl next door, wore her outfit to church. Hathaway went into a rage because she thought Ellen was actually wearing her Easter outfit. Hathaway went next door, beat upon Ellen and tore up the Easter outfit. Hathaway was fighting hard until she fell on a wire protruding from the couch and she got a deep wound near her elbow. She would have that wound for life. Maggie was a outraged with Hathaway; she took out the hidden outfit which had not actually been given away and made Hathaway replace the little girl’s outfit with hers. Hathaway then told all of her little friends that the girl was wearing her dress and hat.

Although she was not of age, Hathaway insisted on following her older brother, Lenard, to school daily. The school allowed her to enter the first grade with the older brother. He was very docile and afraid of the other children. They knew this and would pick fights with him. Hathaway would beat up on them. One day in school the teacher spanked Lenard and Hathaway immediately jumped up on the teacher’s back and began kicking her. Another teacher had to remove Hathaway.

Maggie cried. She didn’t know what she was going to do with Hathaway. What Maggie did not realize was that she was responsible for Hathaway’s behavior. She made Hathaway think that she was better than the other children. Hathaway was developing into a little snob. She did not have to wear the same dress two days in a row. She did not like children who did not have fancy clothes or ribbons. Hathaway’s dresses were made by a local dressmaker who had to keep the dresses hidden from the other mothers for fear they would buy the same material or copy the same pattern. All of Hathaway’s dresses hung on a nail behind the door with a sheet draped over them. Hathaway chose her own dress each day. She was very conceited.

Once, Mrs. Frankie, the dressmaker, had to make dresses for the children who were to be initiated into the children's branch of the Eastern Star. A neighbor saw the material Maggie had bought for Hathaway's dress and immediately bought the same white silk. When Hathaway appeared in a different type material, the lady screamed and cursed at Maggie. Maggie had out smarted her. Hathaway witnessed the scene and was quite pleased with herself. She would not allow the other girl to sit beside her for fear she would wrinkle her dress.

The next day Hathaway made her routine visit to the restaurant and as she watched her grandmother, Maggie, cooking and wrestling those huge pots, perspiring profusely, puffing and groaning, she thought about the dress incident. Again thoughts raced through her mind. One day she would take her out of that hot place, have her sit and she would do all of the nice things for her grandmother: buy her a beautiful home and clothes.

That night as they prepared for bed, after the ritual of beer and shrimps, Maggie fell to the floor. (Mauyea) Elizabeth and Barnes put her to bed and a neighbor ran for the doctor. Maggie had a stroke. When Doctor Elkorin arrived, he examined Mama Maggie and stated that she had a cerebral hemorrhage (stroke).

Her heavy breathing frightened Hathaway. The house was in utter chaos for two days. Maggie remained in a coma. On the third day she began to talk in a slurred voice. She wanted to eat a Hostess cupcake. Elizabeth asked Hathaway to take some of her hidden money and go fetch a package of Hostess chocolate cupcakes. Hathaway sat on the steps and said to herself, "I don't want to spend my money." Just then she thought she heard a voice say, "Just where do you think all of your beautiful dresses and ribbons come from? From your Mama Maggie. How dare you now deny her cookies!" Hathaway suddenly jumped up and ran all the way to and from the bakery. No one was at Mama Maggie's bedside when she returned. Therefore, she jumped up on the bed and began to stuff pieces of the cake into Maggie's mouth. As she stuffed, Maggie blew back. Her breathing was extremely laborious. Hathaway kept saying, "Eat! Mama, Eat!" Elizabeth heard Hathaway and came running into the room. In trouble again! Elizabeth began screaming and asking Hathaway didn't she know Mama Maggie was dying? (How could a seven-year old know when a person was dying?) Maggie died that night.

The following afternoon Mollie arrived from Northern Illinois. She began crying and screaming at Elizabeth and all of the children, especially Hathaway. We had killed her daughter. She had worked herself to death trying to give us everything and now she had died on an old pee stinking mattress. Hathaway knew immediately that she didn't like this little old gray-eyed lady.

When the undertaker came, he had Maggie moved to the front room and proceeded to embalm her. He thought he had the shades drawn but not enough to prevent Hathaway from peeking in. She had observed the whole procedure before the mortician realized that someone was spying on him. Later in life Hathaway told a mortician friend step-by-step how a body is prepared. In those days a mortician embalmed at the house. He had not noticed each time he took the blood to flush down the outside toilet, that Hathaway had followed every stop back and forth to the window, but not before she had learned the basic steps used to embalm people! In trouble again!

After the funeral, Lenard's father came to take him to Detroit, Michigan to live. Mollie took all of the insurance money and told Elizabeth that she would have to leave her no good husband and accompany her to Northern Illinois. Barnes told Elizabeth that he was in love with her girlfriend, therefore, she should go with her grandmother, Mollie. Barnes and the girlfriend took off for St. Louis, Missouri.

Sad and with a forlorn look, Elizabeth and four of her five children accompanied Mollie to a city in Northern Illinois near Chicago.

Mollie had a huge duplex house set up for roomers with a central kitchen separated from her own apartment. Elizabeth and her children were classified as roomers and not a part of Mollie's household. She would furnish their food but it must be cooked in the central kitchen. The insurance money from Maggie was used to remodel Mollie's house. Elizabeth was to clean the roomer's quarters even though some roomers were females.

Mollie didn't trust them to keep their rooms as clean as she would like.

Uncle Joe, after his wife had died, moved in with his mother. He did not like for his mother to treat his sister, Maggie's daughter, and his niece Elizabeth, like work horses or slaves, but he could not deal with his domineering mother any more than could any other members of the family. She knew she was right on every issue. Her slave-driving forces were good to keep people in line just as she had observed her master's tactics during slavery. However, her master had been good to her. She was assigned to the big house. There, she was taught to read and write and all amenities need to belong in a society.

Apparently the master was Mollie's father since she was a mulatto and was treated as a member of the family. Occasionally Mollie would tell Hathaway and Will about slavery and some of her experiences. She stated that when Abraham Lincoln became President and attempted to end slavery, the slaves ran into the street yelling, "Massa Linctum," "We love Massa Linctum!"

Hathaway had to help with small chores. After all, a seven-year old should begin to learn to be productive and earn her keep. The huge house frightened Hathaway. One day she went into a female roomer's room, and to her amazement, saw the female's face and hands were spotted with large white patches mixed in with her brown skin. On the table lay a wig. The lady was bald. Hathaway, screaming, ran from the room, never again to allow this lady to touch her. What Hathaway didn't know was that the lady had a skin disease which she concealed from the public by using a brown liquid to blend the spots with her color, and she used the wig to conceal the baldness.

Mollie learned that Elizabeth was pregnant again. She went wild, yelling and screaming that no bastard would be born in her house. All of her bastards had killed her daughter Maggie. She had cautioned Elizabeth about loose trollops and men about the town and she had defied her. Therefore, Elizabeth had to pack immediately and take the train back to Southern Illinois. Hathaway was filled with joy, glad the opportunity had come to leave this huge haunted house with the woman who looked like a witch. Too, she hated her great grandmother. Hathaway was happy to leave. The joy was short lived and was suddenly replaceed with sadness when Mollie told Elizabeth that Hathaway would have to stay and work to pay for the space her family had used when it could have been rented out for pay and she had lost all that money. Also, pay for the food the family had eaten during their stay in her home.

Too, Hathaway had to be taught that she could not always have her way, she would grow up to be a fool. Maggie had ruined and spoiled her and she was going to break up some of those ways.

Elizabeth did not defend Hathaway. She just began to cry and pack hers and the three other children's clothes. Hathaway began to hate Mauyes, her mother. "Why did Mama Maggie have to die and leave her with all of these mean people?" She wondered. She would never love them. They had better not whip her or she'd kill them. Never in her life had Hathaway been spanked. She had seen Mauyea spank the others, but Mama Maggie never allowed anyone to touch her. Now she had no one to protect her.

The day Elizabeth and her three brothers left, Hathaway hid and cried and begged Maggie to come back and get her. Mollie gave Elizabeth only train fare back to Southern Illinois. When they arrived back there, a friend gave them shelter in a newly built smoke house back of the friend's home. That is where Hathaway's little sister, Paz, was born. The friend took Paz into her home to help Elizabeth out. One brother, Lenny, went with another family friend to Champaign, Illinois. Elizabeth kept Bruce and Marshall in the one-room smoke house. She found day work. Liz, the night prowler, spread the news about town that Elizabeth had returned and given birth to a little girl. Too bad Maggie was not around anymore. The grandmother in Northern Illinois had put her out, sent her back here penniless, on the mercy of the people. Can one imagine the once high and mighty gal when Maggie lived, now coming back poor as a church mouse?

Liz was a jet black woman who wore lots and lots of black clothes, wide brim black hats like a witch, thin spider legs in high top black shoes. Her house was cluttered with junk and black cats. She knew everyone's business. Her one son was very fair-complexioned and could have passed for white. The story about town was that his father was a white man. She was the town's snooper and gossiper.

Mollie breathed a sigh of relief when Elizabeth and her brood left. Now she would go about her business of getting Hathaway settled into her apartment area of the huge house. The storage closet off the dining room under the stairs would accommodate a bed for small child of eight. Also it would be close to Mollie where she could keep an eye on Hathaway. She might just decide to run away. All of the junk in the closet was pushed aside and the cot for Hathaway was squeezed in. No light. That was not necessary.

Will, the grandson of Mollie from Mollie's younger boy, lived in the household. He was the apple of Mollie's eye. Mollie had pampered Will, her grandson, as Maggie had done with Hathaway. He could do no wrong, so why couldn't she be more tolerant and understanding? Uncle Joe understood and did whatever he could to make life pleasant for Hathaway. He observed the difference in characters. Will was mean and vicious whereas Hathaway was outspoken and finished with the situation once she had gotten her point across. She was a fiery little girl.

Every morning when daylight broke, Mollie and Hathaway, equipped with gunny sacks, took to the woods to pick wild greens. These greens were stored in the cellar until Hathaway returned from school. When the planted garden on the lot next to Mollie's home was ready to harvest, Hathaway would have to pick the vegetables, wash and deliver them to stores and private homes. Families would have their meat boiling and call Mollie for a "mess" of greens. They knew the greens would be clean and ready for the boiling pot. To deliver the greens, Hathaway has to cross a river which ran through the center of this town. A couple of blocks from Mollie's home was a dilapidated bridge over the river. When Hathaway had to deliver greens to some of the homes, she was forced to cross this bridge. The bridge would shake and wobble and the waves would flop against it. This frightened Hathaway. Mollie would stand at the end of the block and force her to walk across this bridge.

Weekends, Hathaway would have to wash the bed linens from the roomers and stretch the curtains on stretchers that pricked her fingers raw. She knew she had better not let a drop of blood stain those curtains. By sucking her pricked fingers she learned the salty taste of blood at an early age. If the linens and clothes were not washed clean, Mollie would snatch them from the line and slap them across Hathaway's head and face, sometimes knocking her off of the box she stood on in order to reach the scrub board and tubs. Winter months the linen went out to a commercial laundry. Hathaway was happy when winter set in. During that time she would have to help clean the roomers' quarters. That was a rule in order to live in this rooming house because Mollie did not want rodents and bugs in her place. One had to dispense with privacy in Mollie's rooming house.

Mollie had wall-to-wall carpet on most of the floors and stairs. Hathaway had to scrub these rugs with soap and water. Sometimes the rugs would not dry and the moldy odor made Hathaway sick. Every month Hathaway had to remove the many pieces of crystal from a huge china cabinet and scrub them in a large tin tube filled with hot water and soap. There was no way dirt could have gotten into that cabinet month after month. To this day Hathaway does not care for crystal! She only keeps the precious few pieces given to her as gifts.

Hathaway had begun to outgrow the fine fancy wardrobe Maggie had kept up before her death. Mollie went to a rummage sale for Hathaway's clothes. She now must wear a dress to school three or four days at a time. Hathaway cried and cried. Never before had she worn a dress twice in one week, let along two days in a row! Too, castoff rummage clothes! Never! Maggie was be turning in her grave!

Uncle Joe could not stand to hear Hathaway cry and scream in the mornings when it was time to go to school. He just had to do something. His sister, lying in her grave, would never forgive him for not coming to her granddaughter's aid. He slipped out and bought many new dresses which he kept locked in his room. He made arrangements with a lady to launder them, after which he would sneak them back into his locked closet. Each other day he would meet Hathaway a block from the house and give her a clean beautiful dress to change into at the school.

Hathaway had met a very nice classmate, a boy named Bruce.

Every morning he waited for her to come out of the house and walked with her to school. He took on the duty of standing at the door to the basement where the students had lockers. This way he could keep the other children out of the basement while Hathaway changed into a clean dress.

The ritual was repeated four times a day because she had to change in the morning, change back to rags at lunch to go home, back after lunch, then after school dismissed. Bruce was patient and helpful. At school he taught Hathaway how to ride a bicycle and how to skate. Since Mollie would not give Hathaway two cents to send a letter home to Elizabeth, Bruce would take the letters home to his mother for mailing.

Schools in Southern Illinois were segregated. When Hathaway was admitted to this integrated school, she was given a battery of tests. Apparently she did well on the tests because the second semester Hathaway was double promoted.

Ruthy, a little chubby white girl, became Hathaway's friend and would give Hathaway 10 cents for an ice cream cone at recess time. Hathaway would let Ruthy copy her lessons.

The principal of the school was a very tall lady who made one think of a giant. The gossip among the students was that she wore a wig! Some of the students would do mean things just to be called into her office. They thought that if she spanked them her wig would fall off! Hathaway shared experiences with them about the lady who wore wigs and lived in her grandmother's rooming house.

Uncle Joe thanked Bruce for helping Hathaway. He went out and bought a pair of skates and cautioned Hathaway never to forget to put the skates back in his room so that Mollie would never know. Mollie felt that to ride a bicycle, skate, chew gum and lick an ice cream cone were most unladylike. One day Hathaway forgot and left the skates out near the front porch steps. Mollie just about died. She yelled, screamed, and took the skates away and gave them to her grandson Will.

Occasionally buggy rides on Sunday were scary and stressful to Hathaway. She had a fear of horses and cats. Mollie had attempted to overcome that fear of cats by making Hathaway pick up the family cat. She became so frightened by the softness of the cat that it made her skin pop goose pimples; her hatred for Mollie increased; Mollie's gray eyes made her dislike for years gray-eyed people.

The horse was another animal she could not tolerate, yet on Sundays she had to ride behind him in the family buggy when other people had begun to have cars. The school children would harass her about her crazy grandmother and the buggy rides. They kidded her about such outdated transportation.

Mollie's daughter from Detroit came frequently for visits. Callie was a petite, fastidious person. She brought a small steamer trunk packed with beautiful clothes, scarves and hankies. The likes of those clothes Hathaway had not seen since her fancy clothes had worn out only to be replaced with rummage sale junk. Callie instantly disliked Hathaway. One night Callie went to a neighbor's home to drink and smoke because Mollie did not allow such in her home. Somehow the episode got back to Mollie and it was stated that Hathaway told Mollie. Hathaway never saw her Aunt Callie at the neighbor's home. Callie called Hathaway all kinds of names.

One day Mollie had angered her grandson Will. He knocked her to the ground. Hathaway called her Aunt Callie to come. By the time Callie got to the yard, Mollie had jumped up from the ground. She told her daughter that Hathaway was a liar and that she was forever lying about things. From that day Hathaway swore never to tell her grandmother anything, nor would she try to protect her from her mean grandson Will.

Will was a vicious person. He would cut the scarves on the dresser and swear that Hathaway did it. Every night after supper when Mollie took a nap, Will would try to have sex with Hathaway down on the floor in the dining room. When she refused, he urinated on her and the furniture. Hathaway told Bruce but dared not tell her grandmother because she would say that Hathaway was a liar. He went so far as to put rat poison on her pillow.

The only recreation for Hathaway was an occasional movie. She would have to go with the children from the orphanage. The orphanage was just the other side of the dilapidated bridge across the river. Once when Hathaway accompanied these children to the movies and they were late returning home, Mollie met Hathaway with a switch and beat her all the way home. After that incident Hathaway refused to go to the movies.

Hathaway had to be vaccinated for small pox. The area on her left arm either became infected or she was allergic to the serum because she nearly died. There was fear that the arm might need to be amputated, but she recovered.

A year later Hathaway became seriously ill with malaria. The doctor was stunned because malaria was associated with swamp areas in the South. The doctor encouraged plenty of fluid. Hathaway loved ice cream cones and Mollie allowed her to have the cones during her illness, but when Hathaway recuperated, she had to bite rather than lick the cones. To bite the cones sent chills through her body and teeth!

When Hathaway was eleven and one-half years old, Mollie had to make an emergency trip to St. Louis, Missouri for two weeks. Instead of sending Hathaway home to her mother, she placed her in the orphanage. Some of the children resented Hathaway. They made remarks that she was from that supposedly rich Mollie's home up on the hill; that Mollie thought she was better than other people in the city. Hathaway was called all kinds of bitches. Those who liked Hathaway began encouraging her to fight. Hathaway was too frightened. She had not fought since she was seven years old when she lived in Southern Illinois.

Also, Hathaway had begun to have vaginal bleeding. She did not know what was happening to her. She kept washing her panties and praying to God: "Please do not let me bleed to death" she would plead. One of the older girls saw her washing bloody underwear and took her to the matron. The matron had Hathaway to undress, lie across the bed and began to beat her with a wide shaving razor strap. She kept saying that she was going to teach her a lesson; that she had heard about the name-calling in the dormitory and that her high and mighty grandmother should not have sent her precious granddaughter to her orphanage. She should have sent her to Southern Illinois to her own mother; also she said that Hathaway knew why she was bleeding and that she was an uppity brat.

When the beating was over, the matron had the older girl who had taken Hathaway in to her, give her gauze for a belt, folded rags and two safety pins. The girl showed her how to apply the pack for menstruation. Hathaway's grandmother returned and it took some time for her to recall what menstruation meant.

Hathaway began to evaluate people. The matron had always hugged and kissed Hathaway's grandmother, had eaten many meals in Mollie's home, made over her as if she were made of gold, but deep inside she actually hated Mollie just as Hathaway did. Why didn't Mollie let her go home to her mother instead of placing her in that orphanage? She knew she could never tell Mollie about the experience because she would say Hathaway was a liar. Just as Hathaway never told her grandmother about the shoe repairman, nor about Will every night after supper trying to have sex. Mollie would send several pairs of shoes to this man. He would grab Hathaway up to him and squeeze her tight against his smelly old body. She always told Bruce and Uncle Joe everything. (Later at college Hathaway wrote a debate paper on why she felt orphanages should be closed. She received an "A" on the paper which had been written from actual experience.)

The Skinner family, with many girls and one boy, lived across the street. They always welcomed Hathaway into their home. Occasionally they would tease her about her grandmother Mollie. They stated that Mollie was the "greens" lady, that she felt she was better than the other people.

One of these girls had a birthday party and did not invite Hathaway. When Mollie heard about it she became furious. The next week she had a party for Hathaway and did not invite the Skinner girls. Hathaway did not want the party because it was not right. She liked the girls. Later it only caused her to be teased more at school. Those who came told the others that the house was cold because only one fireplace heated the room; that Mollie was ugly because most or her teeth were missing, and the little fancy tea cakes were hard as bricks.

Every evening after supper Mollie took a nap. Hathaway planned to kill her. In each room of the house there was a fireplace with a poker and other related tools. The day Hathaway attempted to kill Mollie, she had the poker drawn back to crush Mollie's skull. Mollie jumped up and began to scream. The next twenty-four hours were busy with packing. Mollie had sent Uncle Joe to get Hathaway a train pass. She stated she was going to take Hathaway home to her mother because she would come up pregnant. Now that she had begun to have periods, she would begin having bastards like her mother, Elizabeth. Not one word about Hathaway's attempted attack on her life.

Hathaway swore that she would never go to her grandmother's house again in life. Several years later Hathaway did return for her Uncle Joe's funeral and left immediately after the services.

RETURN TO SOUTHERN ILLINOIS

Mollie had Elizabeth meet the train to pick up Hathaway. She herself took the very next train out for Northern Illinois. Elizabeth wasn't too happy over Hathaway's return. She had only one room for the now four. What was she to do? However, in a few months she was lucky to find a two room house. This was a very difficult adjustment period for Hathaway. The clothes her Uncle Joe bought had begun to wear out or were too short. Elizabeth bought her a pair of shoes that had "pancake" soles and high tops resembling those worn in reform schools. Hathaway hated them. Some of the children in school made fun of her clothes and shoes. She retaliated by fighting. Everyday she had to stand before the class with arms stretched out with erasers on each hand. If the eraser fell, the teacher whipped her. The regular teacher had to go on maternity leave. She was replaced with a very young teacher, Miss Chandler.

Miss Chandler was very attractive. Her family were wealthy mulattos who owned the houses and larger farms in this area. Most poor people, white and black, resented the family and passed around derogatory remarks that the family thought they were better than other people in the town and that they were crazy.

People gossiped and were envious largely because the family tended to their business and never bothered with the town gossip.

After several episodes of punishing Hathaway for fighting, Miss Chandler decided on another approach. She told Hathaway after school to come to her house. Hathaway became frightened because the people had said the Chandlers were peculiar people. She would rather take a whipping in school than go to Miss Chandler's house. Hathaway walked around the block many times before ringing the bell. Miss Chandler's sister answered. Hathaway very shyly walked in. The family was having supper.

Miss Chandler had Hathaway wash her hands, sit and have supper. When she had finished the initial serving, the sister asked if she wanted more. Hathaway told her "no." The sister said, "Oh, yes you do," and began putting more onto the plate. She saw that Hathaway was thin and looked undernourished. The food was delicious.

After the meal, Miss Chandler told Hathaway to come with her to the car. As they drove through the town, Hathaway rolled down the window to yell to her classmates on the street, only to make sure they saw her in the car with Miss Chandler. She wondered where they were going. To her surprise, Miss Chandler stopped at the movies; another surprise! Every few minutes in the movie Hathaway would go to the bathroom, only so that her classmates would see that she was with Miss Chandler. When she drove Hathaway home, Hathaway asked her when was she going to punish her for fighting. Miss Chandler answered her by saying, "I thought I would try to help you with a little kindness." Hathaway vowed to never do anything again in school that she knew would displease Miss Chandler. That night she thought about the activities with Miss Chandler. She never had anyone except Uncle Joe and Bruce who had been kind to her since her mother (grandmother) Maggie, had died.

Hathaway found work after school and weekends. She worked for the teachers, a sandwich shop owner and her family who were white. She cleaned, washed, ironed, baby sat and in the summer went to the fields to pick strawberries, beans, peaches and chopped corn. This helped Hathaway to buy clothes and to participate in the social activities at school. She loved to dance and would dance out a pair of $1.98 shoes in a night. Miss Chandler moved the family into one of her larger houses so that Hathaway could have more privacy and a room to do her school assignments.

Hathaway finally helped her mother. She took some of her earned money to buy food for her brothers and sister since Elizabeth only made $3.50 a week. There were times when the children had to wait to eat until Hathaway came home with food she had either brought in from the fields, or the snack shop leftovers, or used her money to purchase food.

She bought buy material from Woolworth's and made dresses for her sister; bathed and dressed her to look nice like the other little children. One day Hathaway washed and pressed her little sister's hair. During the process the little sister's jumping and flinching caused her to receive a small burn on the forehead. Elizabeth was furious! She berated Hathaway and said many nasty things to her. Hathaway ran to the front porch half out of breath but audible enough for her little sister to hear her call her mother a bitch. The sister told Elizabeth but as usual was unable to catch Hathaway because she ran like hell to Miss Chandler. Hathaway vowed to never again try to make her little sister pretty.

Later in life Hathaway forgot the incident. When she became financially able, she bought an educational policy for her little sister.

Hathaway was a stickler for keeping her body and the home clean. There was no money for deodorant or tooth powder. She kept her clothes clean, bathed and used baking soda as a deodorant for body and soda with salt for teeth. Before Miss Chandler came into her life, she would use lard to straighten her hair with a hot comb heated with a wire holder over the kerosene lamps used for light.

Never would Hathaway clean other people's homes and live in a pig sty at her own home. She used orange crate boxes as tables; bed linens were starched with a sheet and pillow cases as top bed spread, and line shelves with scalloped newspaper. Each night she would have to beat her brothers out of bed for getting into bed without washing their dirty feet after having walked around all day bare footed. Too, they would bring in coal and wood for the pot belly stove and drop them helter skelter over the floor. Hathaway would make them neatly stack the coal and wood on newspaper. Water for tub baths had to be heated and every Saturday night she would have to act as a guard, otherwise all three of her brothers would use the same water. When they became older, they began to resent her bossing and beating upon them and began to throw coal at her through the "shot gun" house onto the street.

Hathaway and her mother were never on friendly terms. Hathaway would become very angry with her; when she would come home from work, within thirty minutes the house would look as if a cyclone had gone through it. Hathaway would become very angry; to think all the work done in the house had become torn down in a matter of minutes! She would say nasty things under her breath.

One of the teachers Hathaway cleaned for on weekends became very angry because Hathaway was late coming to her house. She ran into Hathaway's home, snatched up the one and only coat she had given her, took it back and told Hathaway to go to her half-white Negroes and get a coat since she seemed to love them better than she did her. The idea of keeping her waiting until she finished with the Chandler's home. She may be blacker than the Chandlers but she felt she was just as good as they were.

This teacher was a bitch in the classroom. She developed in the students a horrible fear of math. She would beat the inner wrist and hand until the area became swollen if the students did not respond quickly with the correct answer. One day the whole class was beaten; come to find out she was looking at the wrong answer in the back of the book.

It was snowing and cold; Hathaway, wearing only a sweater, ran all the way to Miss Chandler's house and told her what the eighth grade teacher had said and done. Miss Chandler's brother had a loan shop and real estate office on the first floor of their home. She went below and took one of the pawn shop coats from the rack. The coat was an exact fit for Hathaway. It was a beautiful coat with brown fur on the collar and cuffs. Hathaway was cautioned to enter the side door rather than through the front. This way the brother would not know the coat was missing. (Years later when the brother visited Hathaway on the West Coast, he told her he knew that Winnie had taken the coat and given it to her because he could see Hathaway when she passed the window.)

Hathaway wore that coat from eighth grade until she entered Nurses Training 14 years later. She never worked again for her eighth grade teacher. Later in life this same teacher became seriously ill and had only Miss Chandler to help her before her death.

This same eighth grade teacher was angry because Miss Chandler had come to Hathaway's rescue so she tried another way to punish her. A carnival had come to town and Hathaway had won the Charleston Dance Grand Prize of a Five Dollar gold Piece. The teacher was not going to allow Hathaway to graduate from the eighth grade because she had disgraced the class. Nothing but a trollup would dance on a stage. Prior to the Carnival, Hathaway had developed a unique plan. 1) For Halloween, Hathaway purchased material and made a show girl's dance dress. The bodice had small straps and the skirt flared up above the knees. 2) Hathaway had attended the Sanctified Church to learn their members' dance steps. When one male member's head hit the post, swelling began while Hathaway was laughing. The members evicted her. Hathaway had learned many dance steps at school in Danville. When the carnival arrived Hathaway wore her Halloween dress under her regular clothes. When the band struck up "Hold That Tiger" and the stage manager yelled, "Who will join the Charleston Contest?", Hathaway jumped up in the middle of the crowded seats, removed her outer clothing and ran up on the stage in her costume dress. People were awe-stricken with her and so was her brother. When her brother had run home, he told their mother that Hathaway had taken off her dress and was left half naked. When Hathaway arrived home, her mother raised her hand to hit her, and when Hathaway opened her hand that contained the five dollar gold piece, her mother's arm froze into mid air space, then she took away the gold piece. Hathtway never saw it again. Some said: "Your mother bought food with the money. She was not permitted to attend the school's graduation. This was typical action of the people in the area. Miss Chandler's brother who was president of the Board of Education, told the principal that Hathaway would graduate or she would be fired! The principal practically had the stage students to carry Hathaway across the stage to graduate!

Lucy, another one of Hathaway's schoolmates, lived next door. Her stepfather owned the numbers racket. She would take money from the many cigar boxes for her and Hathaway to spend at the school dances. They would pay for the boys who were excellent dancers and those boys would have to dance only with her and Hathaway. Lucy's mother forever boasted about her money. She wore diamonds on every finger but the thumb, which was not fashionable during the thirties. Every Saturday she would move most of her furniture onto the front porch in order to clean her house, only to let the neighbors see her lovely furniture. On Sundays she would wear her lovely clothes and furs down the alley way to church so that Hathaway's mother Elizabeth could not walk to church with her because Elizabeth did not have fine clothes.

Years later when Lucy's stepfather beat her mother after catching her in bed with his cousin, who was a young boy, drove her out of the house, she came to Elizabeth's to live.

Hathaway, who was in the Army, South Pacific area, wrote her mother and demanded she not allow this woman in the house. Elizabeth did not want to put her out but she knew how Hathaway was; she would have the deputy sheriff come and evict the woman. Genny, Lucy and Hathaway were close buddies. They had great times together. Hathaway had not actually experienced sex in a pleasant manner. Will had tried to use her during her stay with her old grandmother Mollie; one of her mother's live-in boyfriends had attempted to show her how men were to make love to her. A neighbor had heard Hathaway giggling with loud laughter and came to her rescue. He was immediately evicted from the house.

One day Hathaway was in a truck with Lucy's stepbrother, Tom. Apparently, he figured Hathaway was involved in sex activities and he wanted to be one of her lovers. Instead of driving

Hathaway home, he drove out to one of his family's farms. He and Hathaway fought in the dust under a large tree. Tom discovered that he had been mistaken about Hathaway but he was not about to give up. Tom took Hathaway in the truck to a nearby small country store and bought a jar of vaseline, then returned to the farm to resume his attempt to have sex with her. He was unsuccessful. Hathaway went to a friend's home to wash her dress before going into the streets of this small town.

The next day a crowd gathered at the sweet shop next door to the school. One of the boys in the crowd was an upper classmate named Robert who was several years older than Hathaway. Hathaway loved him. He knew that she loved him but he considered her a child. Tom told the boys that Hathaway didn't know what life was all about for she had discovered it over the weekend. Robert began to tease Hathaway about being a virgin. Hathaway was embarrassed and decided Robert would be the one to break the virginity stigma.

When the town awakened the next morning, the news was that Robert had been killed in a highway accident. Hathaway went into shock. She attempted suicide by standing in the middle of the highway. Elizabeth could not stand him because he was a mulatto and was a member of the upper class caste system. Hathaway cried and cried for she loved him dearly. What was she going to do without him? She never wanted sex with anyone but Robert and now he was dead before she could have the experience.

Genny and Lucy tried to console Hathaway. They advised her to come with them on their dates. That was no fun. Thereafter she began to cover her frustrations in dancing. School dances were great. Students from neighboring towns attended the dances. One tall handsome boy from one of these towns was an excellent dancer. Hathaway began to flirt with him but his interest was only in being a dance partner.

Sex was never discussed in the home nor in the classrooms, therefore information was exchanged among peer groups. During those sessions those who had experienced what it was, enjoyed shared information.

One night, Hathaway was placed in the same jeopardy as she

had experienced with Tom. The young fellow was known to molest young girls. Hathaway had no interest in him, and when he would not stop his car, Hathaway jumped out of the moving car onto the highway. She could have been killed had there been an oncoming car. She sustained a broken arm.

During the time Hathaway worked for a white family, she checked everything in the house. Nothing was a secret from her. One day she accidentally discovered articles in one of the small drawers of the chest. The articles were powdered and looked like balloons. Hathaway wondered why on earth a person would keep powdered balloons in a drawers.

Hathaway went to her confident, Miss Chandler, and told her what she had found in the drawer. Hathaway was surprised to learn that those things were contraceptives used to prevent pregnancies!

When Hathaway discussed her findings and information with her peers, they laughed at her and asked where would the boys get the money to purchase such things. They too were not familiar with the word contraceptive.

No type of recreation was available for teenagers. Many homes were without electricity to play radios and who had money for a radio? A few of the homes had windup victrolas therefore the gang often met in those homes to learn new steps in dancing. Corn whisky was plentiful for those who were into drinking. Hathaway took a sip and almost choked to death. She told her peers that they were foolish to drink something that was so strong. It burned the throats as it was being swallowed. Too, Hathaway always was in command of her faculties in order to protect herself in any situation. Smoking was not a part of her activities. Hathaway spent most of her time learning new dance steps. She was dance crazy.

Many of the "Hard Shell" Baptist women would shout in church, then mostly married deacons would run to hold them. Hathaway would take notice of the shouting ones, then after church Lucy and she would run down the alley to see the married deacons sneaking into the shouting ladies home. They would sip corn whiskey and party. One day Lucy and Hathaway followed another married woman to meet her lover. When she saw the two following, she reported it to Lucy's and Hathaway's mothers. Lucy's mother beat her. When Hathaway's mother pushed her into a bush of stickers, she began to scream and kick. One of the kicks struck Elizabeth. She sent for Mrs. Watson, the officer who took children to reform school.

Mrs. Watson was happy to have the opportunity to send Hathaway to the reform school in order to get rid of her. Hathaway ran as fast as possible to the Chandler home. (Just as she had done when she was a little girl. When trouble started she would run to her grandmother, Maggie). Miss chandler took the car and Hathaway back to the scene and told Mrs. Watson to get a bus and collect all of the girls, including her niece, who actually was her granddaughter, according to gossip; then she would take them and Hathaway to reform school. If not, then she had better get the hell away from the house. Mrs. Watson sped away for she knew that the Chandler family had more political power then she. Then Miss Chandler talked to Hathaway's mother and the issue was dropped.

Mrs. Watson, the aunt of the girl Tansula, who really was the granddaughter, had the annual Christmas party and always excluded Hathaway. They were class mates but for some reason she never liked Hathaway. All of the girls except Hathaway were invited to the xmas party.

She always rode a tricycle to school and if the air from the wheel touched Hathaway's legs, Hathaway would knock Tansula off her tricycle. Next day in school, Hathaway was punished.

Miss Chandler visited the woman who lived in Mrs. Watson's home. One day when Hathaway walked by the porch at Mrs. Watson it was filled with women and Miss Chandler, Mrs. Watson stated that there goes that bastard of Elizabeth's, she is going to be nothing and have a house full of bastards like her mother. She said it loud enough for Hathaway to hear. Hathaway responded by telling her to kiss her ass. Miss Chandler left the porch, got into her car and caught up with Hathaway. She told her to get in and asked her if she had had a bath. They drove ten miles away to the town with large shopping stores. She bought a complete Easter outfit. First pair of silk hose, high heel patent leather shoes, silk dress, egg shell short summer-like fur coat and an angel shaped straw hat. She told Hathaway to wear the outfit Easter and walk up and down on all of the streets where the blacks lived. Mrs. Watson was thoroughly disgusted because Hathaway's outfit was exactly like her niece's. Only the wealthy people bought in those stores. Hathaway thought about the time her grandmother Maggie had a special dress made for her initiation into the Eastern Star.

One day while Hathaway and neighborhood kids talked in the yard, a man drove up in a new small Ford car. A new Ford Victoria car in the thirties, WOW! The man came up to the group and asked who was Hathaway. Hathaway spoke up and asked, "Why?" "What did he want?" He said, "I am your father." Hathaway stated, "Like hell you are!" They entered the house to confront her mother Elizabeth. He wanted to know why Hathaway had not been told. After the conversation, Hathaway wanted to drive the car. She lied and stated she knew how to drive, almost stripping the gears. He showed her how to drive and guided the steering. She drove up and down all of the streets so that her friends could see. Back at the house, he asked her what did she want. Hathaway told him she needed a pair of shoes. He promised to come the next day to buy her the shoes. He never showed up. His wife was waiting at his mother's home. Hathaway never saw him again until years later when she went to St. Louis to work. She at least knew now who her father was. She and her friends had made fun of a man they thought to be crazy and come to find out this man was her father's brother and her uncle.

Shortly after Water's visit, Hathaway became ill with severe tonsillitis and her menstruation did not appear. She panicked! My God! What is wrong? Immediately she went to see the family physician, Doctor Elkorin. She remembered that he had come when Mama Maggie was so ill and later died. He examined Hathaway and diagnosed her case as severe tonsillitis. The gossip began to fly that Hathaway was pregnant. Hathaway overheard the conversation, was furious and began to dislike her mother more and more. (She had abandoned her at Mollie's. She listened to all of the gossip from neighbors that she was fast and screwing around without ever hearing Hathaway's side.) To the surprise of almost everyone in the town, Hathaway returned to school in a week, never a baby on the scene. Hathaway decided that was it! She would study French, go to college, become a French teacher, live in Paris and never come back to this town.

The doctor had been the family doctor long before Hathaway's grandmother Maggie had died. He recalled the days she had played with his daughter and had observed her growing up into a young teenager. After her tonsillitis cleared, he performed a tonsillectomy.

This contact developed into a very close friendship. Once he learned that Hathaway was interested in French and Medicine, he began to teach her various phases of medicine and the names of surgical instruments in his office. Occasionally she would accompany him on home calls to families living way out in the country.

Some of the upper classmates became jealous that the town doctor had an interest in Hathaway. They told their parents. Gossip began to spread. Someome went so far as to tell his wife that he was dating Hathaway. One of the gossipers was supposed to be Hathaway's friend and when Hathaway went away to work in St. Louis, she asked the doctor if she could replace Hathaway.

He was shocked because he had only been a friend to Hathaway. She had been one of his first deliveries when he arrived in this little town. She had grown up with his daughter. He used to watch them play in his daughter's doll house when her grandmother, Maggie, was alive.

Some of the town gossipers went to his wife and told her that he was dating Hathaway. Later, his wife was accidentally electrocuted in the bath tub. They stated that the wife had committed suicide because of Hathaway.

After her illness, Hathaway returned to work after school. She ironed and baby sat for her high school principal, a domineering person who ruled his family with an iron hand. His wife and children were afraid of him. He did not like one of Hathaway's friends and stated she was too wild and common. He did not wish her in his home. Hathaway had seen this girl's mother shot though the neck by her love. She felt sorry for the girl and befriended her. Also she was Hathaway's neighbor and classmate. Hathaway knew how it felt to be rejected by her peers. The friend was a mulatto with skin that resembled "chicken skin." The kids said it was that way because she bathed with washing powder. (Later, this very principal abandoned his family: wife, two children, his job and ran away with this same girl. Years later he burned to death and the girlfriend escaped.) The principal told Hathaway that he wished she would apply herself in his science class as she did in French. In geography, she only knew where to find Paris: some day she would visit the place.

Hathaway loved French. She would learn the vocabulary far ahead of the assignments in order to speak only in French. She was ridiculed by her classmates. They were not interested in her showing off and they did not comprehend.

Her French teacher was a mulatto who could not tolerate blacker people. However, she had Hathaway to do her ironing every week. Often she had told Miss Chandler that she was crazy to bother with Hathaway because Hathaway was nothing but trash, would only bring shame to her, have a house full of bastards like her mother, "like mother, like daughter." At the end of the semester she flunked Hathaway in French. Hathaway ran to the principal's office and used his phone to call Miss Chandler who was now teaching in the high school in a town six miles away. Hathaway, crying, told Miss Chandler that the French teacher had flunked her. Miss Chandler told Hathaway to pack every damn book she had and leave when school was dismissed. Her homeroom was in the French teacher's room. When the French teacher saw Hathaway with all of her books on the desk, she asked "Why?" Hathaway told her she was taking them all home in order to study "just a little bit harder" as she had been advised. Hathaway never went inside the school again. This teacher's plan was to force Hathaway out of school, make her become a whore about town so the people could say, see, we told you she was nothing. But God takes care of babies and fools. Hathaway was not a baby but a young girl trying to make it. She could not understand why blacks were so cruel and mean to blacks. Things would have been different for her if her Mama Maggie had lived, but she was determined to make it, come hell or high water. God helped her through life by guidance and aid from Miss Chandler and her family.

Miss Chandler not only moved Hathaway and her family from the one and half room house to a three-room house so that Hathaway could have more room, she also provided clothing, food and weekly allowance for her work in the Chandler home.

She picked up Hathaway daily and took her to the high school where she taught. French was not taught, only Latin. Hathaway attacked Latin just as energetically as she had French and won a weekly prize. Hathaway participated in all school activities and, since her former school and the present one were severe rivals, she was often in verbal fights with the former school kids. After all, she still lived in their town.

In the new school she was a member of the choir. Each year all of the schools participated in track and intellectual competition. Hathaway was one of the four who sang "Marquita" and won first prize for the school.

Students and teachers were observing the basketball competition. The French teacher who had flunked Hathaway and caused her to leave said, "We never knew that you could sing; you could have been on our team." Hathaway told her, "No! You people in that school were too damn dumb and mean to give a person a chance! Miss Chandler slapped Hathaway and in a low voice said, "I have told you about cussing!"

Hathaway learned many things from the Chandler family. One incident occurred that helped her to develop honesty. Large amounts of money were always around in the sister's room. Hathaway began to help herself to the money, thinking that it would not be missed. Miss Chandler approached her and retrieved the money. She left a saying with Hathaway: "He who bits shall be bitten, only harder." Never again would Hathaway so much as take a penny if it were on the floor.

Some of Elizabeth's friends became very jealous of the help from the Chandler family. They began rumors that the Chandler family was just using Hathaway because she was black and since mulattos really didn't like blacker people. Hathaway had it out once more with her mother. After all, the aid was given to the whole family and not Hathaway alone.

It seemed as if Elizabeth and Hathaway were never compatible: never a conversation. In the new school where Miss Chandler taught, Hathaway became very close to a classmate named Bertha. She was very intelligent and excelled in math. Hathaway's fear of math from her grade school experience prevented her from comprehending algebra principles. She copied algebra from Bertha. The principal knew this and told Hathaway. Of course she denied the accusation. By the same token, Hathaway was charging another classmate 25 cents to copy from her other assignments. His father was a doctor in the area. Bertha's family owned a farm. Frequently Hathaway went home with Bertha. Her family welcomed Hathaway and treated her as a member of the family. Hathaway had never seen so much food at one setting. The fried chicken was delicious. When the girls wen upstairs for bed, Hathaway had almost a whole chicken to eat. When Bertha spent nights with Hathaway, she would cook pork chops since Bertha had her fill of chicken. The visits to Bertha's home took Hathaway away from an unpleasant atmosphere. Bertha's mother was a lovely person. Love and family life in their home was wonderful. Those pleasant visits with Bertha's family would never be forgotten. After school, Hathaway was either up at Miss Chandler's house, Bertha's home or attending gossip sessions with her peers. Many weekends were spent dancing all night. She would attend the sanctified church to learn new dance steps. Hathaway liked acting and would entertain her peers. When they left a movie, Hathaway would reenact each person's part in the movie. She would mimic each one of the teachers in the classrooms. One day she would teach and act exactly as Miss Chandler in the classroom.

Before the last semester of high school, Hathaway had completed requirements to graduate. Therefore, she was permitted to go to work in the strawberry fields in order to purchase her graduation clothes. She and Miss Chandler obtained brochures from several colleges. Hathaway was interested in obtaining a degree in French and preferred to attend the same university from which Miss Chandler had obtained her degree. The tuition was more than Hathaway had imagined. It would have taken years to earn that amount of money for tuition. Miss Chandler asked her how had she planned to attend college when she had no money. Hathaway told her that she would find a way and as soon as she graduated, she would go to St. Louis, get a job and save money for college.

They checked another program in hair dressing, but Hathaway was not interested in cosmetology. Nursing was not too expensive. One could train in a three-year program for one hundred eight dollars. Too, nurses' programs would enlighten her more about Maggie's illness and death. She could do nursing in order to obtain money to attend college for teaching credentials. She always wanted to teach in the classroom like Miss Chandler. Often Hathaway would hold her peers attention by mimicking Miss Chandler in the classroom. Miss Chandler went beyond academic responsibilities. She encouraged students to set priorities, develop a healthy image of one's self and practice hygienic principles. She also taught students how to survive in larger cities that had more to offer than their small town. She advised the graduating class to stay at a YMCA or YWCA when they arrived in the cities where no relatives were around; seek employment at Urban League and, with a sample phone, she taught students how to use the phone directories.

Later when Miss Chandler left the high school and became principal of an elementary school, she took the whole student body on trips to larger cities to dine in fabulous restaurants and to tour educational facilities. It was during her assignment as principal that she wrote the song, "I Am Somebody" in the 1960s. All of the students learned the song. The song has a copyright. A mirror was placed at the entrance of the school and at the side of the mirror was posted the song, "I Am Somebody." When the students entered they could look at themselves in the mirror and say "I Am Somebody."

One day Hathaway shall be just like her! Just wait! Another one of her quotes to Hathaway's class in economics was: "Mene Mene Tekel Upharsim" - (Thou art weighted in the balances and found wanting) which is exactly what happened to Hathaway. She flunked the economics course. Miss Chandler had warned her time after time to do her homework. Just because she befriended Hathaway gave her no right to try to get by on friendship, This was another lesson learned from Miss Chandler.

The day after graduation, June 1934, Hathaway, with a Woolworth pasteboard suitcase and twenty-five dollars from Miss Chandler, hopped a vegetable truck going to a St. Louis produce market. This little Southern Illinois town exported its vegetables to St. Louis. The driver of the truck had grown up with Hathaway's mother, Elizabeth, and father, Al Waters. He was happy to have company. Miss Chandler had given Hathaway the twenty-five dollars and instructed her to get a room at the YWCA and go to the Urban League to seek employment.

The town gossipers had a field day. Hathaway had gone to St. Louis to prostitute. She would return with a house full of bastards like her mother. Hathaway felt that most the people prayed that she would carry out their prediction. (Later in years when she saw the movie, "Zorba the Greek," the section where the old women squatted around waiting for the lady to die, then picked her room bare in a few seconds, reminded her of those old gossiping biddies in Southern Illinois. Hathaway vowed to never again live in her mother's home nor this Southern Illinois town.

When Hathaway arrived in St. Louis, she called her father. He came down to the market and informed Hathaway that he had not told his wife that he had a daughter. Therefore, she would have to get back on the truck and return to Southern Illinois. Hathaway began to use Southern Illinois Levee Camp profanity on him and told him to go to hell, return to his wife because she had money to live on while she looked for a job. She didn't need him. He had lied to her about the shoes when he first told her that he was her father. She had managed all these years without him and she could continue to live and make it without him; that she planned to work to earn one-hundred eight dollars to enter nurses' training. He attempted to slap her for cursing him. The truck driver told him that he would beat him to a pulp if he touched Hathaway; that he didn't have the decency to say that she would take a train or bus back home. No!, he ordered her to get back on the truck. Hathaway told him in no uncertain terms to go to hell and get lost. He began to cry and Hathaway told him that the more he cried, the less he pissed. That's what people had said during her young days. He began to have a change of heart and asked her to forgive him and to come with him. He had a lady friend who would help her to find a job.

Hathaway accompanied her father to the lady friend's home. She was a big fat jolly person and appeared quite impressed that Waters thought enough of her to bring his daughter to her. That night as Hathaway and the lady lay in bed, she told Hathaway about her love affair with Waters, but for some reason he had not been by lately. She heard that he was now dating the maids in Clayton, Missouri. Hathaway was tired and wanted to sleep.

Waters had a maintenance contract with suburban Jewish home owners in Clayton, out from St. Louis. His clientele was tremendous. Consequently, he had a staff of six men to help maintain the area. His wife was an excellent cook. Between the two they lived quite well during the depression.

The next day Hathaway went to the Urban League, sat all day before a call came for a maid without a reference. A Jewish family in University City, Missouri, wanted a young person to be more or less a companion to their young daughter. Hathaway was hired that day for fifteen dollars per month. No experience was required for the job.

The apartment was small, one bedroom with a closed-in sun parlor used as a bedroom for the small daughter. Hathaway had to sleep on a cot in her room. This meant that when the family entertained, Hathaway had to wait in the kitchen until the guests left before she could go to bed.

The man was much older than his wife. In order to have extra money, the wife would bake and sell sponge cakes at Famous Barr Store, and knit clothes on order. She taught Hathaway how to knit so that while she sat in the kitchen awaiting the guests to depart, she could knit on the article to be sold.

The job was exciting. Never before had Hathaway eaten Jewish foods. The lady taught her how to cook capons, chop live, gilfilte fish, borach, etc. The complex was a huge apartment building. A brother to this family lived on the second floor. The two brothers owned a poultry market. Consequently, they had capons, chopped livers and egg dishes most of the time.

Hathaway's father would come by to visit. He would have different girlfriends in his car. He was financing the college career of one of these girlfriends at Lincoln University in Springfield, Missouri. She won a prize as the best dressed girl on the campus, yet here was his daughter who needed only one-hundred eight dollars to enter nurses training. He spent over one-hundred eight dollars a month to entertain his girlfriends. On one occasion he borrowed eight dollars from Hathaway's fifteen dollars per month. (He died owning Hathaway.) Hathaway had to wear white shoes dyed black, sweaters under spring coats; yet he blantantly exposed her to his well kept mistresses.

Occasionally Waters took Hathaway out for a drive and eventually introduced her to his group of married friends who accepted his mistresses. He impressed these people by providing large quantities of food and liquor and, of course, graced their houses with his fabulous new cars. Hathaway observed all these activities with disgust. He was a leading deacon and treasurer of one of the Baptist churches and never missed a Sunday from church.

Finally, Waters told his wife about having a daughter in town. She called Hathaway and invited her for a Sunday dinner. She wanted to see if there was any resemblance between her husband and his supposed daughter. When Hathaway arrived, the meeting went along fair but strained. All hell broke loose when she stated Waters had told her that Elizabeth was older than he and had taken advantage of him. Hathaway began cursing her and Waters, then, a fist fight began between the two of them and Hathaway ran from the house and vowed never to return.

For the next few months every Thursday, maid's day off, Hathaway attended the operas in Forest Park. Waters, with a change of heart, returned to visit Hathaway on the job. By now Hathaway was dissatisfied at work when what started out to be pleasant became burdensome. Every morning at 6:00 a.m. She had to prepare breakfast for the master; 8:00 a.m., prepare for the wife and daughter, Marguerite, bathe and dress her for school; clean, wash, cook, wash windows inside and out every week. If the family ate dinner with relatives above, then Hathaway would have to serve and wash the dishes. Never was any money given her for knitting on the sold garments, yet she would have to bank the money and keep the book for her employer because she did not want her husband to know that she was making outside money. She planned to divorce him at a later date. He was too old for her anyway.

She gave Hathaway outgrown clothes of Marguerite's to send to her sister. When Waters found a job with a family in Clayton and Hathaway left to accept the new job, the lady wanted to charge her for cast off clothes. Hathaway told her she was not working for cast off clothes. Hathaway told her she was working for money to use to enter nurses' training, therefore, she'd return the clothes. The lady allowed her to keep them.

Hathaway in alternate months sent fifteen dollars to Elizabeth to help her and the kids and fifteen dollars other months to Miss Chandler to apply to her tuition of one-hundred eight dollars needed to enter nurses' training. Slow progress!!

Waters helped Hathaway to change jobs. The new job in Clayton was much nicer: a Jewish family of five in which the father was owner for a nationally know lingerie company.

Hathaway was paid twenty-dollars per month salary to assist with cooking which ended up with Hathaway doing it all and cleaning the house. Living quarters were in the basement. The room was supposed to be safe but Hathaway's wrist watch was stolen. Her brother, Lenard, in Detroit, had given her that watch when she was in the eighth grade. As Hathaway now reflects on the past, she was very lucky. She could have been a statistic in that basement.

The wife traveled quite a bit with her husband on out-of-town business. Her mother was quite old, therefore she left Hathaway in charge of the house. The oldest son was attending the University of Washington to become a doctor which he did not wish to be. His parents were pushing him. To take the pressure off her, the mother asked Hathaway to encourage him at intervals by explaining to him why an education was important. With all of the advantage and money he wanted no part of it. He was interested in music and would serenade Hathaway with Claire DeLune.

Waters began to let Hathaway drive his car providing she bought the gas. His wife became tolerant and had her over to the house. She attempted to amend her early rejections and turned out to be a fairly decent person. Hathaway began to have pity for her as she observed how unfair Waters was to his wife.

Hathaway began to meet young people in the area and in St.

Louis. Her love for dancing continued with visits to the Bellmon Waiters Club and parties at home on Bell Street for big band musicians and after hour dances. She made friends with many young people in the areas near Clayton. One of the girls was a student nurse. One of the boys in the group became a doctor. Several were students at Lincoln University. Men became interested. One older man became so infatuated, he wanted Hathaway to run away with him. Never on his life! Hathaway had only one plan: to have a limited amount of fun, then forget it and focus on nurses training to become a professional, independent person.

By sleeping in the basement with the dampness from the walls, Hathaway became very ill. Waters had his physician to see her but would not pay him. The physician's diagnosis was severe bronchitis with asthmatic tendencies. Hathaway called long distance to Miss Chandler. She immediately drove to St. Louis, paid the physician and drove back to Southern Illinois with Hathaway propped on pillows. Hathaway's Jewish family was sad when Hathaway became ill. They gave her a two years supply of lingerie as a gift when she left for nurses training. Contact continues with this family today.

Hathaway, now 18 1/2 years old, had worked a year and a half and by alternating the money between recreation, Elizabeth, and the nurses training fund, she still needed more than one-hundred eight dollars needed to enter nurses' training. The Chandler family went into conference.

Miss Chandler told Hathaway that she felt Hathaway now knew the value of a dollar and, since she was determined to go to college or nurses' training, the Chandler family would see to her being admitted to the nurses training school in September. She had three months to recuperate before leaving for school.

The Chandler women packed a steamer trunk with everything a girl needs at college. The day Hathaway left, one of her brothers had a convulsion, so Elizabeth was busy with him and the doctor. Consequently, only the Chandler women saw her board the train. None of her friends came to bid her farewell. Later Hathaway learned that most of them were jealous. The adults again began their malicious gossip. Well, Hathaway didn't become pregnant in St. Louis, but she will; just wait, fast as she is, she will become so by one of those doctors. Miss Chandler instructed Hathaway that if anything ever happened, do not contact anyone but her; that she would help her through any situation. Miss Chandler gave Hathaway enough money to stop in St. Louis to have her hair styled and obtain a manicure which she had never in life had before!

MID WESTERN TOWN - 1936

Hathaway was overwhelmed and excited when the taxi stopped at the hospital. She said a prayer of thanks to God for his guidance and help through Miss Chandler and family. She had made it. No way would she let anything stop her now!

The superintendent of the hospital knew Miss Chandler and her family because he taught in the school where Hathaway had graduated before becoming a physician and had advised Miss Chandler to have Hathaway come early to the hospital. By being early she would be the senior of her class. The matron was a tall buxom woman who had been a matron at a girls' reformatory. Her voice rang and sent chills through a person. She scared the hell out of Hathaway!

She taught Hathaway how to make her bed in the huge dormitory and gave her a quick orientation session. As senior of the class, it would be Hathaway's responsibility to orientate the rest of her classmates as they arrived. Eighteen students arrived one by one that day. Once they were settled in, a call came for the class to assemble downstairs in the classroom. When Hathaway joined the others in the room, they were shocked to learn that she was their classmate. By her officiating in the dormitory, they thought she was a senior student nurse assigned to assist them.

The first year of training went very quickly. Hathaway did

exceptionally well academically. The exposure from her doctor friend, paid off. Miss Chandler was quite pleased with her progress and had her grades printed in the local Southern Illinois newspaper in order to show the people there that Hathaway was on her way to break down their predictions and gossip.

Everyone now wanted to get on Hathaway's band wagon. Mollie, like Paul Revere, spread the news in the Northern Illinois town that her great granddaughter was in nurses' training. Letters and packages began to flow. Never before had there been any contact after the day she took Hathaway home to her mother except when Uncle Joe died. Waters told all of Clayton and St. Louis people that his daughter was in nurses' training. His wife even sent a package for Christmas. At vacation time, she and Waters came to drive Hathaway home. Out on the highway Waters asked her to give him her train fare so that he could buy gas. Hathaway told him to stop his damn car, let her out and that she would walk back to the train or bus and go to southern Illinois alone. He relented and drove on.

Several people in Southern Illinois began to talk to Elizabeth. They became interested in Hathaway's progress, sent greetings and stated that they were so proud of her, since so few girls had left there for college and Hathaway was the second one to ever enter nurses' training from their town.

Hathaway's attitude toward most of these town people never changed. However, her attitude toward Elizabeth changed. It was because of her training in the maternity ward. Hathaway had never seen the birth of a baby. She was assigned to watch a patient after the doctor explained that the patient had not dilated enough, therefore he and the scrub nurse were going to dinner. A few minutes after they had left, all hell broke loose. Hathaway then knew what Elizabeth had suffered when she brought her into the world. Hathaway vowed to make it up to Elizabeth. She would give her the nicer things in life that she had planned for Mama Maggie.

The first year of training was exciting; getting to know the classmates and adjust to the routine schedule of nurses' training. Students had to be in the dormitory by 8:00 p.m.. Nevertheless the students found ways to beat the restrictions.

After the students became settled in the dorm, exchange of activities before entering training was topic for discussion. During these sessions, some began to learn how to smoke. Students were required to attend chapel every morning before reporting to duty. Hathaway seldom made chapel on time. When the director checked students' finger nails, uniform, scissors and nail files in the uniform pocket, she noticed that Hathaway was beginning to become too hippy and needed a girdle. She was fitted and had to purchase the girdle. It was a Charis type made of staves. The Charis type girdle made Hathaway into a robot because the staves would not bend with body movement. This provided an excellent excuse for Hathaway when she was late for chapel: girdle trouble! After a year, the director told her she had lied on the girdle long enough. All of a sudden Hathaway developed diarrhea. That lie stuck for only a few months. The director told her that if she had diarrhea that long, she would be too weak to work.

Hathaway soon learned that the training school was a method to obtain students to staff the hospital. The separate black and white hospitals were integrated by an underground tunnel.

Some of the staff people in the training school program were just as vicious as some of the Southern Illinois people. One day one of the supervisors stopped Hathaway with an intern on their way to change a patient's dressings. She approached Hathaway with the statement that the school should require a full photo of students instead of a bust type, then students with a shape such as Hathaway's with a big protruding butt could be eliminated. Hathaway told the supervisor that she could get a girdle to hold down her butt but she couldn't do anything about her hanging lower lip. The supervisor wanted to slap Hathaway but the intern had witnessed the episode. In retaliation she gave Hathaway hell when she did her practice in the operating room. She would use pick-up forceps to pinch into a student's kin. One day during an operation, she pinched Hathaway. Then she began to cry, and the whole field had become contaminated. Hathaway had to be replaced in the field. When she was in the shower, the supervisor entered and told Hathaway that she cried only because she could not curse her out in front of witnesses. Later Hathaway diagnosed her as a sadistic bitch.

In spite of the adverse reactions from some instructors, there were sincere instructors and staff who saw to it that the students received excellent training. Hathaway's class was involved with a patient who had been diagnosed as having Sickle Cell Anemia. Their pathology book contained only four pages of description for the disease. The most fascinating part was when they examined the patient's blood samples under the microscope. The red blood cells instead of the normal oval shaped resembled a sickle shaped like a curved metal blade with a short handle. In order to receive the normal amount of oxygen into the body, red blood cells must be round. The patient was very appreciative of his nursing care, therefore requested Hathaway's class to assist in the performance of an autopsy just before he died.

The dietician attempted to flunk Hathaway but Hathaway had news for her. She practically memorized the whole book. This dietician was very mean to most of the nurses. During Hathaway's term as president of the student body, they all went on a strike against the dietician.

One of the supervisors had given Hathaway a 95 for her class experience, but after the feud with the dietician, who was her best friend, the supervisor changed Hathaway's grade from 95 to 75. Hathaway immediately took the incident to the superintendent of the hospital. He had the supervisor to reenter the grade of 95. When this dietician became seriously ill, Hathaway was assigned to be her special nurse. When she recovered, she cried and asked Hathaway to forgive her for having been so mean to her. Hathaway was enjoying her training and outside contact too much to be concerned about the few unscrupulous supervisors.

One evening a group of students attended a jazz session in one of the theaters where famous bands of musicians were appearing. After the sessions, the group met in a private home for an after party. It was at one of these parties that Hathaway met Hubert. Once again life became exciting. Many pleasurable evenings were spent with Hubert. His mother was quite pleased and tried to have Hathaway become a permanent member of her family! No she thought! Never!! No way, Jose'!

Students developed ways of getting around the 8:00 p.m. curfew. The morgue room windows provided an escape route. The students would take bags of clothing to the laundry room next door to the morgue on pretense of doing their laundry. Upon return to the hospital, the laundry bag was dampened to make it look as if it contained wet clothes.

Hathaway and her group always had a classmate who attended early Mass services so that in the event they were caught coming in late, they would say that they had attended Mass. One night about 3:00 a.m., when Hathaway and her buddies were sneaking in, a classmate lost her shoe. Her mother had recently sent those shoes which cost twelve dollars, a lot of money during that period. The classmates burned the other shoe so that it could never be mated with the one the matron picked up.

Most of the students had not seen a home of ill-repute and the red light districts where women used knocks with metal knockers on the windows to entice men to come in for a night of fun. This area was located near the heart of the town. One of the presidents had a haberdashery in this area, President Truman, of the U.S.A.. All of the things in life that were not discussed or blantantly exposed in some towns were observed. They began to hear and learn about lesbians and homosexuals. A group of homos owned a night club and had fabulous floor shows. It got back that a group of students were at this night club. The mother of one of the guys became a patient at the hospital. During visiting hours the supervisor who used pinching forceps on the students in the operating room sat at the desk in order to observe whether or not the guy spoke to any of the students. To whom he spoke she thought, would give her a clue as to who had been seen at the club. Word spread quickly that he was on the floor. The guilty ones almost suffocated in the closet while awaiting visiting hours to end!

The superintendent of nurses tried to use con strategy by having Hathaway come to her room at nights to brush her long hair. Once in the room she would try to intimidate her by asking which student had done this or that; who had danced in a night club wearing her basketball suit with the hospital letters on the back of the shirt. Hathaway was the captain of the team, and told her that all the students had returned home immediately. She did not say how immediately after the game because Hathaway was the guilty person. In fact, almost all of the things the superintendent of nurses had asked about, Hathaway was the person who had done that particular crime.

A number of students were relatives of many of the world renowned big jazz band men. When the musicians came into town, they would have their nieces or cousins meet them for the famous Bar-B-Q in the city. They roomed in private homes and were not supposed to have females in the rooms. One night they took the students to one of the large sitting rooms that was next to a bedroom. They all sat in a circle on the floor and were eating Bar-B-Q. All of a sudden the bed fell in the next room. There were snickers but Hathaway became hysterical with laughter. No one could shut her up. It was 3:00 a.m. In the morning, so the landlady evicted every one of the band members. They were ready to kill Hathaway. Twenty years later in Europe, when Hathaway introduced her husband to Count's men, one of them spoke up and said, "Man, does she still laugh at the wrong time?" It so happened that her husband knew about the incident.

Several of the students and Hathaway enrolled in a ballet dancing school. Hathaway loved to dance and this was another activity to keep her and the classmates busy. They were quite active at the YWCA and at playing basketball. Hathaway never learned to swim during their visits at the Y. Hathaway attended the church services as often as possible. The services were not as emotional with shouting, screaming, knocking over benches as the women had done in her small home town. Too, she didn't know the people as well as those hypocrites back home.

Jam sessions with some of the classmates would keep an outside listener in stitches. One of their classmates would share a few of her intimate secrets at this particular session. She asked them if they had ever had their bell rung; everyone said, "yes". When the session broke up, several asked each other what the hell was she talking about.

Hathaway was elected president of the student body. She was quite surprise and pleased; surprised because she felt that many of the students did not approve of her outspoken manner. Perhaps that was one reason she was elected. Too, she had been elected as the outstanding student of the year. She received an award given by Ms. Staupers who at that time was one of the Administrators of the Colored Graduate Nurses' Association. This organization was developed because black nurses in the 30s were not accepted into the white American Nurses Association. The award was a gorgeous blouse that Hathaway wore for a number of years.

Many problems existed at the time Hathaway was elected president and the past president would not become involved. Students resented being treated as children, such as curfew at 8:00 p.m. The dietitician would not allow night nurse students to eat noon meals. They would have to attend classes from 9:00 a.m. to 12:00 noon and could not eat!! That was the last straw!! The students thought it was time to strike in order to make someone listen to their complaints. The list of complaints we written.

Hathaway called the superintendent and told him that it was imperative to attend. He stated that it was impossible. The majority of the students voted to strike and composed their demands. That night Hathaway and another schoolmate slipped out to alert the press. The next day, reporters were there on target; no one ever knew how they got the message. The probation students were not allowed to participate because it would have been detrimental when they were evaluated for acceptance into training. Of course the administrators were outraged and wanted to expel Hathaway. The students stood out! They would have to expel all of those who had participated. The whole situation was closed and training continued.

Hathaway had to deal with the political situation in training. She had assisted with voting in her home town, but, not being of age, had not actually voted. It was mandatory that all students vote as directed. Since Hathaway could not challenge the process, she could void the ballot by marking every square. Later she learned that it had not mattered one way or the other because the machine was rigged. This was the era of political corruption. It took years for Hathaway to develop a positive attitude toward politicians and politics.

Hathaway's love affair with Hubert began to become serious. His mother planned many activities to introduce Hathaway to people in the community. Hubert enrolled in a southern university band. Before Hathaway could adjust to his being away, he returned. He stated he was not interested in college. This attitude was more than Hathaway could tolerate. Consequently, he and Hathaway began to have frequent verbal fights. Hathaway began to anticipate the time for graduation, which would give her a wonderful opportunity to get away from Hubert.

Word came that Mollie, now ninety-eight years old, had been in a car accident. The door had flown open and she was thrown out of the car. She wanted to see Hathaway. No Way! Hathaway had vowed never to see that lady again. Hathaway sent the money for Elizabeth to go. Aunt Callie had survived the accident and now this. She never forgave Hathaway for such treatment toward her mother, Mollie. Hathaway told the family that she could not be deceitful toward anyone regardless of who, relatives and all. Never pretend when one knows the inner-self has a negative feeling toward that individual. Hathaway had been reprimanded many times for being so outspoken without regards for other's feelings. Once she had gotten her point across she was finished with the issue.

Several months before graduation, Hathaway had to work on the maternity ward, and a patient came in for delivery. The patient named Hubert as the father of her child. Hathaway was dumbfounded. When she saw Hubert, all hell broke loose. He tried to convince Hathaway the pregnancy occurred during the time of one of their falling out periods. Like hell it did; he had been seeing her all the time he was dating Hathaway.

Later the young mother had Hubert arrested for child support. Hathaway's classmates forbade her to ever speak to him again. Hubert's mother was excited over the grand-baby and began to lighten up the pressure for his and Hathaway's marriage. Hathaway never had planned to marry in the beginning, especially when he refused to attend college. She had plans to go much higher into nursing education than a three year diploma registered nurse. Three years of training was completed.

Throughout the three years of training, Miss Chandler kept Hathaway in clothes, watch, coat, glasses, monthly allowance and all of her graduation clothes. Elizabeth came to Hathaway's graduation. Waters did not so much as send a card. It really didn't matter. It is difficult to explain the wonderful feeling one has when one walks down the aisle and receives that diploma. Hathaway wished that all of the Southern Illinois people could have seen her.

Once a student graduated without any makeup time, she had to move out of the dormitory immediately. Miss Chandler sent Hathaway money to rent a room until time to take the State Board Exam.

Beside review sessions for the State Board Exam, Hathaway and her friends partied every weekend. The landlady became jealous of the activities and, too, she was not asked to participate. Therefore, she complained to Hathaway that she had too much company in and out daily and they were running up her water bill by using the bathroom too frequently, consequently she would have to move. Hathaway and her buddies laughed and laughed; they had never heard of anything so ridiculous in their lives. Fortunately, Hathaway had finished the examination and was leaving immediately for St. Louis to await the returns.

ST. LOUIS

In St. Louis, Hathaway moved in with her father. She could not work as a nurse until the State Board Exam grades were out as to who passed. In the meantime Hathaway needed money. Therefore she returned to maid services. This time around, being a maid was really comical. Some of the ladies at the luncheons given by Hathaway's employers would ask, "What kind of nurse are you, doing maid's work instead of working in a hospital?" Hathaway would answer by saying that one had to eat to survive in this world and for them not to worry. This was only temporary because she was awaiting the State Board Returns.

One lady did not want to call Hathaway by her real name because the neighbor's daughter had the same name. Never before had she heard such an odd name before and she thought it was a fairly new name. Hathaway told her that she was nearly twenty-three years old so it had to have been around quite some time. Next day the lady received a call from a friend she was to have met in the downtown area. She told the friend that she had hired a new nigger and you know how they steal, so she had better stay at home. Also, the nigger is driving a better car than hers.

That day was laundry day. Hathaway went downstairs and

put all of the clothes of various colors plus the throw rugs and jammed them all into the machine, pushed the button, went upstairs and demanded her pay for the time she had worked past and present days. She had the dust mop with her and when the lady began to scream that she didn't have any money, Hathaway told her exactly where she kept her money, so get it and pay! The lady told Hathaway that she was going to call the police. Hathaway told her to call and before they could arrive, she would have beat the hell out of her and then await their arrival.

Hathaway became very nervous while waiting for the State Board report. Every day she had a headache. Then her watch was stolen from the desk in her bedroom. She swore and be damned that her father had taken it to pawn. Then she thought about the one that disappeared four years ago from her basement room. He was a maintenance man for that building. Miss Chandler had given her that watch because she needed one with a second hand during her nurses training days. Too, he was still into his love affairs with the maids in the area and needed quick money all the time.

Everyday Hathaway waited for the mail. One classmate had written all who had failed and not a word about her and two other classmates. The suspense was killing her!

Finally the letter arrived. Hathaway opened the envelope with very nervous fingers. All she read was "We wish to congratulate you!" She read no more; she fell out into the floor and began to cry.

The next week, Hathaway was hired by one of the hospitals in St. Louis. She and a classmate shared a room next door to the hospital. Hathaway rekindled old friendships from nurses' training days and began to meet new people. She began dating and was enjoying life when a letter came from friend. The friend wrote that Hubert had contacted her and since Hathaway had not answered his letter, he was coming to St. Louis to find her and marry her. His mother called that he had gone out of his mind and, what had Hathaway done to him. Hathaway told her that no way would she marry her son, she should have him marry the mother of his child. After a while he settled down and married the girl.

Hathaway and her classmate began to party and go out on

dates. One of the doctor's brother at the hospital began to like Hathaway. In the meantime Hathaway was dating a guy who worked at the "Y." She thought she could handle two dates at a time. One night she went out with the hospital guy and when she returned home, the "Y" guy was waiting on the steps. He followed Hathaway into the house, took off his belt and began to beat her as if she were a child. Her roommate jumped out of bed and ran to the hospital and got into one of the nurse's beds there, leaving Hathaway alone to fight her own battle. After that, Hathaway refused to ever see him again.

The hospital guy was very handsome. He had a friend who wanted to double date. Hathaway introduced him to another schoolmate nurse. The two married and, to date, are still very happy. Hathaway was really becoming interested in her new boyfriend because he entertained her so royally every weekend. Everyone thought that wedding bells would be ringing soon but Hathaway knew better. She had received a letter from her mentor and supervisor during her student Public Heath nurse training and she was told that the department wanted her to return as a staff member. Hathaway was really in a quandry. She told her boyfriend of the news but she hadn't decided on which steps to take - stay or return to the Midwest town where she trained.

Hathaway did not have to ponder the situation too long. Her boyfriend took care of it for her. The following weekend the local black newspaper contained an article in the gossip column that stated: "What temperature taking lass had to have her temperature taken after her lochinvar boyfriend on his white horse swooped down and fled the scene with his hash swinging chic and later they were married across the border?" Boy! Did the doctors at the hospital ever tease Hathaway with funny and derogatory remarks.

A couple of days later Hathaway's public health mentor came to tell her that the job was waiting for her. She had come by train since she could travel with passes. Once again Hathaway came away from the problem smelling like a rose, just as she had experienced all her life. She submitted her resignation and began preparation to return to the city where she had trained as a nurse.

Hathaway told her mentor that she would arrive that weekend for the new position as a visiting nurse. Later she called her schoolmate and told her of the plans and asked that she not tell anyone because she wanted to surprise everyone.

When Hathaway arrived, she called the cab company that they had all used during their training days. Here she was back, in the town she had left only six months ago. The driver drove in the opposite direction from the address Hathaway gave. She told him that she knew the way since she had graduated from the hospital and he was not going where she had asked. He asked her if she knew a young man name Hubert. She stated yes. He continued to tell her that Hubert had informed the company to have whoever picked up Hathaway to bring her to his apartment. Hathaway did not wish to make a scene. She would settle the issue with Hubert, also she could have slapped her friend for telling him that she was returning for a job there.

Hathaway was in no mood to deal with Hubert. She was only interested in going to her mentor's home, resting and reporting for duty Monday morning. When she confronted Hubert, he explained that he moved out of his and wife's apartment weeks before she arrived, and they were no longer a married couple, that he wanted Hathaway to forgive him and for them to begin their once-upon-a-time happy relationship. Finally after hours of discussion, he promised to pay child support to his ex-wife, and he would not pressure Hathaway into marriage once the divorce was final.

Hathaway settled into a room rented from a neighbor next door to nurse, B. Lee, her mentor. This way she could ride to work with B. Lee. The landlady was an elderly lady with a hearing problem. She was happy to have a nurse in their home because her deceased daughter was a nurse and had been a supervisor in the hospital where Hathaway had trained.

Hathaway felt that she was at last on her way to accomplishing her goals; with a salary of $100 per month which was the highest salary at that time for nurses, she could easily save toward college; just a 3 year diploma was not enough knowledge. Another one of her schoolmates was also hired. The two really worked hard in their districts. They became an asset to the department. The number of families in their districts increased tremendously. The Director was quite pleased.

Hathaway and her friends began to party every weekend in one of the other's homes. In Hathaway's home, the landlady would retire early into her second floor bedroom and, with a hearing problem, she could neither hear nor see what was happening below.

The affair with Hubert became a disaster. Hathaway began to date other men. She and her group continued contact with the musicians they had met during nurses' training. One night at the routine weekend jazz sessions, Hathaway met one of the doctors who was interning at the hospital where she had trained. He loved her style of dancing and was surprised when he learned that she was a nurse. He thought she was a professional dancer. He and Hathaway began dating. Hubert became very jealous and tried to make trouble. She and Doctor CM had a very enjoyable relationship for quite some time.

When the two began to feud, Hathaway could not bring herself to say what was bothering her; she never drank whiskey but this particular time, she held her breath and took a big swallow of bourbon. She felt the whiskey would give her courage to say just what was on her mind. Did she ever pay for such an act! That Sunday night she became absolutely drunk and when she went to bed, a nightmare dream scared the hell out of her. She literally crawled into bed with Mrs. Hamilton. The landlady, Mrs. Hamilton, treated Hathaway as if she were her daughter. She would cook delicious meals: hot rolls, pies, cakes, etc., for all of Hathaway's friends.

The position with the Visiting Nurses Association was far more interesting and demanding than when Hathaway was a student. She was delighted because she had chosen Public Health as her choice of nursing during her affiliation. Hathaway was assigned as a field teacher for the affiliated students from her training school. The districts were segregated. However, when Hathaway was inadvertently given a white family, she became friends with them and, when the supervisor called them to apologize for the error, the family asked that she continue to give them service. Their request was granted. The director was very pleased because she had really wanted the services to be integrated.

Several of the affiliated students knew Hathaway before she graduated. Some had even partied with her, consequently, a couple felt they did not have to apply themselves. Hathaway counseled them and explained that friendship and requirement of knowledge did not mix in the training. One must have knowledge when applying Public Health principles; grades could not be given on the principles of friendships. One student would not listen, consequently Hathaway flunked her. The word got around; no more trouble thereafter.

In Mrs. Hamilton's home, a couple rented one of the other bedrooms. Several months later, with the need for more privacy, Hathaway moved into an unfurnished apartment. It was time to begin developing credit status. Some of her schoolmates had apartments and between all of them, there were parties every weekend, pot luck food, bedroom furniture taken down for dance sessions, with live music whenever the big band musicians were in town.

Many people about town became envious of the groups' activities. The superintendent of nurses became very angry because they were hired by the health department instead of the ones she would have recommended. She went so far as to write a letter to Hathaway's director that they partied every night and were not the type for public health positions. The director was very pleased with Hathaway and her classmates' work, therefore she discussed the issue with Hathaway, had her read the reply that she did not have jurisdiction over the employees after working hours and that the districts' census had increased from their excellent work. Hathaway mailed the letter to the Superintendent of Nurses at the hospital.

Several of the married nurses lived in the community. One thought that Hathaway was just a little too fast for her, therefore she never had Hathaway in her home. Later in life she changed her opinion - Why? Hathaway never knew.

Wayne, who was a handsome journalist had spent some time in Hathaway's home town and when he moved West, Miss Chandler asked him to visit Hathaway. The two became close friends. He was an excellent dancer, was just what the doctor ordered when Hathaway wanted to make Hubert and Dr. CM jealous.

She would have him escort her to many of the formals. He would hold her close and dance cheek to cheek as if they were lovers. They won the Kappa Alpha Kappa Crown and Sweetheart title at one of the formals. Their actions would blow Doc and Hubert's minds. Most of the women who had ignored her became very charming in order to meet her very handsome escort. Hathaway would talk with them, then very politely walk away without an introduction to her handsome friend.

In spite of Hathaway's conniving ways, she and Doc continued to feud. It was brought to her attention that he was also dating another young lady. The aunt of one of the schoolmates had a formal dinner party for her. Hathaway and Doc were invited. After the dinner he told Hathaway that he had to return to the hospital because he was on duty. Liar! No one on duty ever left the hospital. Hathaway refused to allow him to escort her home. She took a cab home, changed clothes, called Hubert and went to the movies. Floor shows featuring Jay McShand's band followed the movies. When the lights came one, there sat Doc and his lady friend in back of Hathaway and Hubert. The two became furious and began quarreling with each other. The young lady ran out of the movie and Hubert practically dragged Hathaway out, he was so angry. He stated he was finished with her for good.

The next episode was more than Hathaway could take. One afternoon when Doc CM was visiting her, one of her schoolmates came in. Hathaway went into the kitchen and when she returned, they were kissing. Shortly after that he began dating the schoolmate. It was rather difficult to let go, but she had no alternative. It was evident that it had been a one-sided affair. He really only liked her dancing talent. It seems as if Hathaway always dated guys that her schoolmates wanted. She had witnessed the same thing with Hubert and one of her other schoolmates. The same things had happened during high school days.

One day Dr. CM's roommate met Hathaway and asked if he could occasionally join the crowd at the weekend parties. He was invited to attend the Thanksgiving affair scheduled to be at Hathaway's apartment. At the last minute, plans were cancelled. Hathaway forgot that he was to come until the doorbell rang and there stood Dr. GR. Hathaway wasn't really interested in seeing anyone, especially some one close to Dr. CM. They had to go out for dinner because Hathaway had not thawed a thing to cook.

Before the breakup with Dr. CM, Hathaway occasionally would go to the hospital and they would have lunch. In the beginning, she tried to keep her relationship with GR on a platonic relationship. Pressures from all sides began to close in. Hubert continued to be demanding. He became irate and told her that he had done everything she requested before she would resume their relationship when she returned to the city. Every month he had to give her money for child support which Hathaway mailed to his ex-wife. He had done everything to prove his iove; NO! She had shunned him for the doctor's, who knew nothing about love. She had used him!! Dr. CM began to date her schoolmate and now Doctor GR had begun to pressure her.

Hathaway took stock of what was happening in her life and felt it was time to move on. On the job, the Director had told her that a stipend was available to attend the University of Minnesota School of Public Health summer sessions.

In order to supplement the stipend, she had to obtain a loan from the Urban League. This was the second time the Urban League had come to her rescue. It was through the League she had obtained her first job as a maid in St. Louis; now it had come through with a loan to attend the University. She made preparations to leave immediately; all of the guys were stunned. Doctor GR came to the empty apartment and found two suitcases in the middle of the room with Hathaway awaiting the cab to be taken to the train station. He became furious that she would make such a move without telling him. He had no idea that beside wanting to pursue a degree in Public Health, this move gave her an opportunity to get away from all of her bad love affairs - it seemed as if that was the story of her life.

Summer in Minnesota was exciting. The people were very friendly and entertained the students most royally. Most of the friendships continue today. Classes at the University only whetted the desire for more learning. Three other schoolmates also attended the summer sessions.

A new treatment for polio victims was developed by a Sister Kenny from Australia. the University of Minnesota endorsed the treatment and students from all over the United States came for summer sessions on the new wet pack treatment to extremities. Hathaway's schedule did not include Sister Kenny's courses. With her inquisitive mind, however, one day she audited the class and met Sister Kenny.

Hathaway's schedule kept her too busy to write any of her boyfriends. Just one week before she left school, she wrote Doctor GR. She was not aware that he and Doctor CM had been recruited into the Army Medical Corps and had been sent to Fort Huachuca, Arizona.

When summer school ended, Hathaway returned to her Public Health Nurse position. She became the first black Red Cross Army Nurse Recruiter in this Mid-Western City.

Elizabeth came to visit and was surprised when GR's brother, Doctor Sam, met her at the station and later that day, he took her to dinner while Hathaway completed plans to have Elizabeth's teeth fixed. The surprise was a shock to Elizabeth but all went well. When Elizabeth returned home, many of the women rushed to the only Negro dentist and demanded their teeth be fixed like Elizabeth's. When the dentist saw Hathaway, he asked her if she could have more dental work done on her mother and thanked her for creating a sudden increase of patients into his office.

World War II had begun to accelerate and the need for Army nurses, especially Black nurses, increased. Hathaway was adventurous and, now that she was the recruiter for Black Army Nurses, she decided to join the Corps in order to see the world. Further, all of the eligible men were being recruited. When Hathaway approached her Director and stated she planned to join the Corps, the Director was stunned. She told Hathaway that she was classified as essential on her job and to think before making such a drastic move. Hathaway's mind was made up and she definitely was going to enter the Nurse Corps. In her young days in high school, she had dreams of going to Paris. Speaking French had been one of her greatest desires in life. She never forgave her high school French teacher for interrupting that desire.

Hathaway's Director and Mentor, B. Lee were sorry to see

her leave but extended their best wishes. Hathaway left immediately for a physical examination at Fort Lenardwood, Kansas. All went well until weigh in time. She was overweight but was accepted after signing a waiver for the few pounds over the normal weight. After the acceptance, she was granted a leave prior to her reporting for duty. In October, 1942, Hathaway entered the United States Army Nurses Corps as a 2nd Lieutenant.

Hathaway went home to visit before taking off for camp in Arizona. Elizabeth and the town people were excited when they saw Hathaway in uniform. She walked with pride all over the place.

Beside wanting to show off her uniform, Hathaway had plans to make Elizabeth's house beautiful and comfortable; no more cleaning lamp globes, but to Hathaway's disappointment, Elizabeth refused to have electricity installed. She was afraid of it. However, new furniture, draperies, etc. were greatly appreciated. Hathaway arranged for her dress shop to send Elizabeth clothes regularly, especially for birthdays and holidays. An Army allowance would provide a comfortable life that would not necessitate her doing day work. Hathaway encouraged Elizabeth now to take life easy; dress well; travel and do her own thing.

Just before Hathaway left for camp, one of Elizabeth's friends came to visit. She immediately began to find fault with the type of furniture, the fabric, the colors, and asked Elizabeth why she had bought this, that, etc. Hathaway became very profane with the lady and asked that she leave with her jealous mind. Elizabeth became very angry with Hathaway and stated that these people in this town were her friends and she had to live here. Just as it had been all of Hathaway's life, never a mother-daughter relationship, no matter how hard Hathaway had bent toward having at least one happy ending. Hathaway told her "to hell with those phony ass people" and left immediately for the camp in Arizona.

Hathaway took the train from Southern Illinois to the Fort in Arizona. She learned a lot more about segregation than she had ever witnessed in Illinois. She had grown up in an atmosphere of segregated schools, theaters, restaurants, but had never seen signs, "colored only - white only."

Maybe she and her peers had been too busy enjoying life to notice. The train had sections for colored only in the back of the engine of the train cars. Finally the trip ended in a desolate section in the desert. The station was dilapidated and the night was pitch black-scary! Thank goodness there were other Army people getting off. An Army weapons carrier type vehicle met the train.

In daylight, the physical aspects created a different impression. The Fort was practically surrounded by mountains. There were two hospitals called #1 for Negroes and #2 for Whites. There were the same numbers of the hospitals where Hathaway had trained in the Midwest - only difference was that the numbers had different translation and no underground connection. The blood for Army use was marked Afro so that it would not be used on white soldiers. Number 1 Hospital was completely staffed with Negroes.

Just outside the Fort at one of its many gates was a village called the Hook. Here were rows and rows of green one-room houses to be used for prostitution. What a health hazard - no running water - no type of sanitation. A couple of miles down the road was the Mexican Border. The sunrise and sunset were the most beautiful skies Hathaway had ever seen.

A few days after arrival. The Chief Nurse took the new recruits on a tour of the Army Hospital. What a surprise when Hathaway entered the Dental Section. There stood Dr. GR. He gave out a shriek over seeing her. He told her that only a week ago, before he had married his college girlfriend; Oh! If he had only waited, then he could have married her. Hathaway said no way could he have married her. She congratulated him and moved on.

The word moved fast that Hathaway had arrived. Late in the day Doctor CM came to the Chief Nurse's office to greet her. The other guys who had either trained in the same hospital or worked with her in the St. Louis Hospital decided to have a welcome party for Hathaway.

The party was about forty miles from the camp at the home of Captain and Mrs. Boyd. Everyone was partying down. Hathaway had to report for duty the next morning and everyone was too drunk to drive that night. Next morning, they were still knocked out from hangovers. When Mrs. Boyd finally drove Hathaway back to camp, she was absent without leave (AWOL). She was put on house confinement for five days. All of her buddies took turns to call her on the phone every night.

When Hathaway was taken off punishment, she visited only the wives on the Fort; never again would she go off camp without her own transportation. One of the wives on the Fort was from Hathaway's home town. She had married a doctor and he had been assigned to this area. They had a car and it was at Hathaway's disposal whenever she wished to use it. After the attempted rape by Tom in that little Southern Illinois town, she had vowed never to leave home without money for bus fare. The Army AWOL issue was not a matter of money but lack of transportation because everyone was too high to drive her back to camp. She would not be in such a predicament again. She would limit her visits to friends who lived on the Fort. At least she could walk back to the barracks if a problem developed.

Hathaway's brother and several other high school friends were stationed at the Fort. Hathaway would, in her civilian clothes , attend the dances at the noncommissioned officers club. It was just as if the good times during high school days in Southern Illinois had never ended. Hathaway danced her heart out. The high school boy she attempted to have as a boyfriend but was only interested in her dancing now wanted to become her boyfriend, even told her that he was her first boyfriend. Hathaway laughed in his face and told him he knew that it was forbidden for an officer to date an enlisted soldier. Oh! How she loved the opportunity to tease him!

It was at this Fort that Hathaway saw Bruce, her long lost friend who had helped her through the sad times when she lived with her great-grandmother, Mollie. Bruce had become a doctor. The two reminisced over there childhood days. He was quite pleased to learn that Hathaway had made it to this stage of life. He felt she was on her way now and congratulated her on having finished nurses's training. Bruce was in the quarters to pick up his date. When she saw Hathaway and Bruce embrace, she became very indignant and began to tell off Hathaway. She was in for a rude awakening when Bruce told her that he had known

Hathaway most of their lives. Today, she laughs about the incident.

A couple of months later while visiting one afternoon with her friends (Army wives) at the officers club, a very handsome 1st Lieutenant walked in. He sat at the bar and began to stare at Hathaway. She thought he was really staring in order to develop a bond between the two so that she could introduce him to one of the civilian ladies. He sent drinks over to the table, introduced himself at Lt. E.C. Templeton and began a conversation mostly directed to Hathaway. A famous orchestra was scheduled that night at the officers club. He asked Hathaway if she had planned to attend with a date or not. Hathaway accepted his invitation. When Lt. Templeton arrived for the date, he was a most handsome man in his full dress uniform. He reminded Hathaway of Wayne, who used to help make her boy friends jealous when she lived in the Midwest. Some of the nurses in the quarters practically fainted when they saw him and began to make snide remarks about Hathaway being so short in stature, kinda plump with a big ass; how did she capture such a handsome hunk?

Within six months the affair was mushrooming into a very fabulous affair. Every Sunday after church they had dinner at the officers club and the lieutenant always had a beautifully wrapped gift beside Hathaway's plate.

Lt. Templeton had graduated from a Catholic University in LA. He had been an assistant to the priest. His voice was deep and melodious especially when he read poetry. He used this expertise to woo Hathaway. Their evenings ended with his reading beautiful romantic love poems. Hathaway shall never forget his favorite, "This My Beloved." Also, he was an excellent dancer. He and Hathaway would team up with visiting celebrity dancers at the officers club. One night they were dancing with one of the famous celebrity dancers Fadit, Nichols, and when the Lt. threw Hathaway to him, their hands missed and Hathaway fell flat on her behind. She bounced up and kept on dancing. Later Hathaway learned that the officer she married had witnessed the episode before he knew her. He was observing the dancing from the balcony.

Just as the ending of a year's happy and most loving moments together, Lt. Templeton proposed to Hathaway. He gave her a gorgeous engagement ring. Although they began to make preparations to marry, Hathaway had inner conflicts. Was this what she really wanted? He was so handsome. The snide remarks from her co-workers made her wonder, does he really love her? A guy this handsome wants to marry her. Then she said to herself, Hell, I am just as beautiful a woman as he is a handsome man. Yes, I'll marry him. We should have some beautiful children.

The wedding date was set and the two began to comply by the Army rules for marriage. In order to get married one had to obtain permission from the Army. Approximately twenty-five forms had to be cleared to prove that neither one already had a spouse back home. This screening was done by the Army Red Cross Department.

By his being Catholic and Hathaway a Protestant, the Catholic Church required signed papers that if there were children during this marriage, they would be reared in the Catholic faith. They requested the required forms from the Priest which had to be sent to them. In the meantime they proceeded to sign documents for Hathaway to be his beneficiary. Hathaway's mother was her beneficiary and the lieutenant did not wish that Hathaway change this.

In the midst of all the planning, awaiting for approval from the Army and the Priest, a new contingent of officers arrived at the Fort. The hospital's Commanding Officer issued an order for all nurses to come to the officer's club that night in order to meet the new officers. When the Chief Nurse came through the barracks, knocking on doors and yelling the Orders, Hathaway became very angry, defiant and stated that she was not going to obey the order, that she had entered the Army to nurse the ill and wounded, not to serve the men's desires nor would she promenade before the officers to allow them to pick the woman they wanted - same as slaves on a block; Hell No!!

When Lt. Templeton came for her, she told him of the episode and that she would not go to the club that night. Instead she took off all of her clothes and jumped into bed nude. She was so damn angry; the idea of such an order!!

Within a couple of days, Hathaway's name headed the list of

nurses to be sent with a hospital cadre to the South Pacific in the jungles of New Guinea. She was fit to be tied. Hathaway did not take the assignment as a punishment, which it most likely had been intended, she wanted to travel but not at this particular time because her marriage was still in the planning stages and awaiting approval. After the marriage, then she would be ready to travel abroad. All the plans had to be placed on hold because immediate training for overseas began.

Lt. Templeton and Hathaway were devastated. Why did it take so long to clear the forms? Each night ended with their crying in each other's arms. They made a vow to keep in touch and to marry as soon as the hostilities ended.

The night before departure, he came to the barracks to help Hathaway and co-workers pack their footlockers by the Army method of rolling clothing. When clothing is rolled tightly, more articles can be packed. The next day, the group gathered at the train station to depart for the West Coast. Lieutenant presented to Hathaway a beautiful bracelet that contained a miniature picture of himself with an inscription that said, "God Bless Thee Dear and Keep Thee Until We Meet Again." Hathaway still has that bracelet to this day.

When Lt. L.H. saw Lt. Templeton and Hathaway clinging to each other and in tears, he assured Lt. Templeton that he would look after Hathaway's well being. Hathaway was very sad throughout the trip to the West Coast. Lt. L.H. attempted to soothe her as much as possible.

The group went to a port in California for most training. This time the training was on how to ascend then abandon the ship. The deck was thirty-feet high and one had to ascend by using a rope type ladder. They were taught to push with their feet. Hathaway did not follow the instructions. Instead of pushing, she was pulling up and about half way up her arms gave out; too much weight for the arms. There was a musette bag packed with emergency supplies strapped on her back. The climb became too stressful. Her khaki slacks around the buttocks and ankles had ballooned out similar to Turk's clothing. One soldier on the ground began to take pictures of her front and behind that looked as if she had been blown up.

Lt. L.H. and another officer told Hathaway to hold on and the two scaled the rope ladder to her rescue. That was the beginning of LH looking out for her welfare as he had promised Lt. Templeton.

That night Hathaway removed all of the articles from the pack on her back and filled it out with Kleenex. The next day she made the trip up the ladder by using the pushing with feet and light weight pack.

The light weight pack was a good idea since the group had to march five miles to the ship. Everyone was settled on the ship. The first day out, a blimp guided the ship out into the ocean. Lt. LH told her that it was only a guide and once the ship was on its way, the blimp would return to California.

Hathaway just about died from fright. She did not know how to swim and she was frightened of water. This fear had developed at the age of eight when she had to live with her mean great-grandmother, Mollie, who made her cross the river on a dilapidated swing type bridge with waves thrashing against the bridge.

The troops had to "stand by" daily at 6 A.M. and 6 P.M., in the event there was an attack and one must abandon the ship. Lt. LH told Hathaway not to panic and that he would help her if they had to abandon ship. Every drill session Hathaway made it over to his side. Years later Hathaway lamented, what a fool! To believe that Lt. LH could help her in seven miles of deep water. He would have done well to save himself in a shark filled ocean. Nevertheless at the time, it gave her confidence and a secure feeling. Each day, Hathaway took her shower and changed the clothing that she wore until next shower time. Never would she be caught in PJs and have to abandon the ship! She began to read the Bible with comprehension. During all the years of mandatory church attendance, she had never paid attention to the minister nor the teachers. She only went to church to show off her pretty dresses with large matching ribbons. She was a demon. Every Sunday in church, she would embarrass Elizabeth. The toilets were outside and since Hathaway had a fear of the toilets, she would urinate in her clothes and the urine could be heard dripping onto the wooden floors!

Hathaway thought about all this and her mockery! How she used to entertain her peers by mimicking the minister with his white handkerchief to wipe away the profuse perspiration from his face and going down on his knees as he shrieked about seeing his mother approaching on a cloud from heaven. (This remark would invariably create a chain reaction from the audience; shouting would peak); or he would say, "I heard a voice telling me to preach the gospel." Elizabeth would become so provoked with Hathaway for calling the minister a liar because if he heard a voice he would have killed himself running.

The ship's motions did not cause Hathaway to become seasick as it did most of her comrades. They could not tolerate food and since the food was so delicious, Hathaway would help them to the dining room to get their food. The sight of food would make them sick; then Hathaway would take their food, especially when the menu contained turkey and dressing with lots of cranberries.

The ship was traveling in a convoy and after a few days out at sea, the enemy's submarines picked up the sound of the convoy. The hospital ship was taken out of the convoy and zig zagged eighteen days across the Pacific Ocean to Australia. It was later learned that a couple of the ships in the convoy were destroyed. Soldiers who had trained with the hospital unit went down with the ships. Hathaway and others had known these soldiers.

Finally, after eighteen scared days, a special navigator had to meet the ship and bring it safely into the harbor of Sydney. After seeing the beautiful harbor with banks of flowers that extended almost into the ocean, one could understand the need for the special navigator.

When the unit was allowed to disembark, many Australian people came to the dock and stared. Some attempted to feel the behinds for tails. The ignorant ones claimed they had been told that the Negroes were wild with tails like monkeys. The unit stayed in Sydney for a couple of weeks, then was transported by train to Brisbane. This city is known as the Gold Coast, with beautiful coastal beach areas. In the beginning, Australia had been an undeveloped country used to exile criminals from England with the idea no one would survive.

At that time, Aborigines inhabited the country and they were supposed to have been driven from their land into areas further away, similar to the treatment toward the American Indians.

The Aborigines were not allowed into the lucrative and productive land that was world renowned for its production of wool that made it the world's largest export country of wool. Hathaway was now grateful to her first Jewish employer who had taught her to knit. She began to knit garments for all of her friends and those who had children. She knitted sweaters and dresses and one dress separately for her mentor, Ms. Chandler.

The Black nurses were housed in a segregated barrack at the end of the staging areas for all nurses as they awaited assignments into combat areas. Hathaway and the other fourteen nurses were awaiting the completion of their hospital in the Melina Bay area off the Coral Sea. All of their hospital male staff had gone ahead to supervise and assist in building the hospital for a two-hundred fifty bed capacity and, if necessary, expand to 500. The ship with the male staff enroute to Milina Bay, New Guinea, became ship wrecked on one of the reefs. That episode caused the delay in arrival.

During the interim, the nurses explored the city. Hathaway attended church services and one of the young ladies invited her to accompany her home for dinner. This family made a practice of having all of those in uniform to come for Sunday dinner after church services. This activity gave Hathaway an opportunity to meet different soldiers and officers from different countries. There were four young girls in this family. They are now adults with families of their own. The mother is deceased but the daughters continue to maintain the friendship.

The Black soldiers were victims of segregation. The non-commissioned officers' club was located in the prostitute area of the city which had no paved streets. They were refused services in the restaurants. Hathaway and a couple of the nurses decided to take care of the situation. No services could be denied an officer. Therefore the nurses sent home for money, met with the soldiers to obtain a list of places that refused them services, and with the list, they went into the restaurants. After many displays of this type action, the Australians began to develop a different and healthier attitude toward the Negro soldiers. The NCO Club was moved out of the slum area. Hathaway and her group took out membership in the YWCA, attended the leather craft classes and all other activities the YWCA had to offer.

The local newspaper printed an article about the Negro nurses. The article contained a statement that Hathaway was a student at the University of Minnesota. The Australians knew that Sister Kenny's new wet pack treatment for polio victims was accepted by the University and that she was one of the instructors. Brisbane was her home. Immediately her relatives and friends came to the camp area to meet Hathaway. They came in a long black chauffeured car and created excitement when the chauffeur asked the white nurse officer on duty to please have Lt. Hathaway come to the office. After the relatives visit, Hathaway was on a roller coaster! They took her every place.

Hathaway asked the relatives if she might divide the fifteen nurses of her unit into two groups and pay for the expense to expose them to all of the places they were taking her. They were delighted but refused money. Some stated that the contact was enlightening since they had never had contact with professional Negroes.

Women from the "Y," clubs and interested families came forward to meet the nurses and entertain them in their homes. This contact with the Australian families has continued with Hathaway and two other nurses. They returned for a visit in the seventies. That marked thirty-two years after it all began.

Hathaway and her buddies would stop the Australian soldiers to ask for directions just to hear their accent which was similar to England's cockney twang. They learned that "bloody" was not a nice word. They developed a friendship with the Dutch Air Force pilots and Javanese soldiers.

This friendship allowed them an opportunity to observe the culture of people from different countries. One of the Javanese soldiers, Lt. Jackmon, became interested in Hathaway and in that short period of time, he wanted her to marry him and go live with his family in Java until the war ended. He stated his culture did not approve of premarital experience and that he loved her dearly. Hathaway told him that she was engaged to Lt. Templeton,

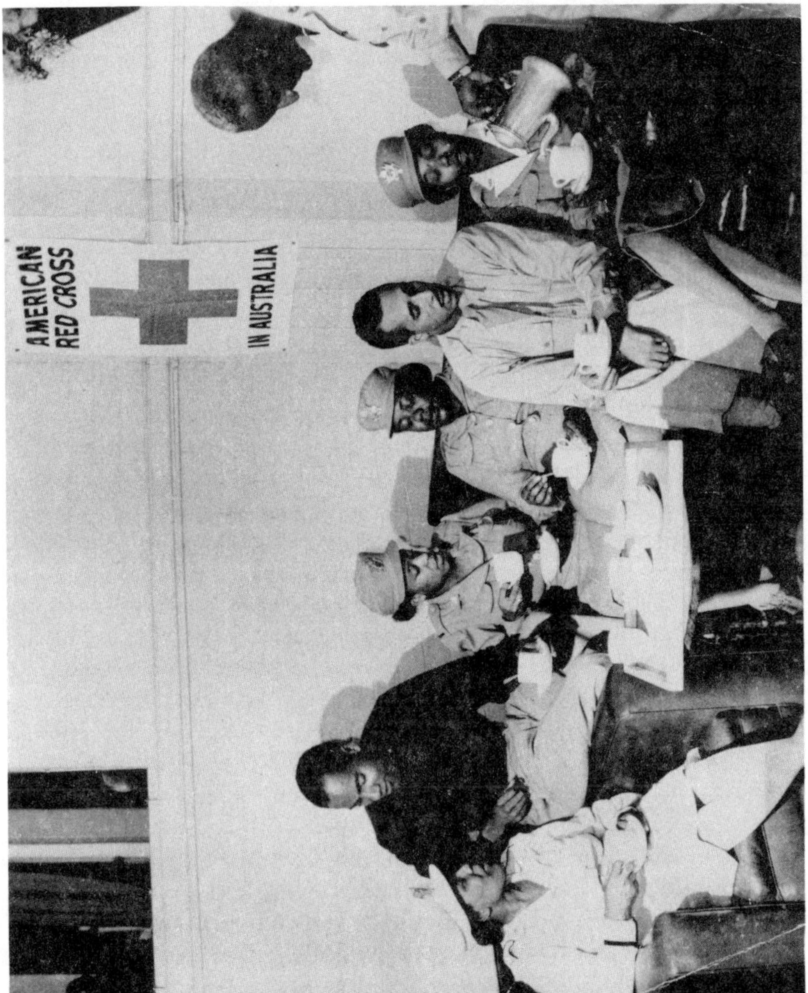
AMERICAN
RED CROSS
IN AUSTRALIA

her one and only love, and whatever gave him the idea she was romantically interested. After the war ended, he wrote Hathaway, asked her to consider his proposal and please come to Java. The War Department forwarded the letter to Hathaway's address. She and her husband had a big laugh over it. He said, "See what flirting will do." At the time Hathaway and her buddies were being inquisitive and only wanted to know how other people lived. They did not realize the guys would become "carried away" over platonic friendship. This friendship exposed Hathaway to different kinds of Javanese foods that she had never heard of - curry seasoned meats, pickled eggs, bits of meat on a skewer - each person dipped his skewer of meat in a sauce that was shared with everyone around the table. Desserts were fantastic and delicious. The Australian foods were not too different from American dishes. The crumpets and tea served during afternoon hours lent a bit of royal atmosphere. Hathaway had never cared for kidney pot pies or stew when she was growing up.

One lady invited Hathaway and two of her comrades for dinner. When they arrived, Hathaway noticed that small pillows were on all of the chairs except one. Hathaway knew the significance, therefore she immediately sat on the chair without a pillow. The lady turned red and let out a groan. Hathaway asked if she were ill; the answer was No. Therefore Hathaway answered for her by saying, "You thought I might injure my tail, huh!" The lady was embarrassed but admitted she had been told that Negroes had tails. Hathaway told the lady that she had no knowledge of anatomy and human development and if she had a tail she has enough adipose tissue to protect her tail. The lady apologized but Hathaway had her comrades leave and they went to a restaurant for dinner. The comrades asked Hathaway why she would not stay for dinner. Hathaway told them–no way. She might have served heathen food!!

One Sunday Hathaway accompanied her comrade, who was Episcopalian, to church. The service was absolutely beautiful. There were two choirs facing each other chanting the songs throughout the service. This was Hathaway's first experience in attending church services that offered so much solemnity. She was deeply impressed.

A couple of the Australian women took Hathaway and her buddies on a trip to the Zoo which was on an island and accessible only by a ferry boat. The weather was extremely hot. When the group arrived and approached the concession area, they were seated and made very comfortable. A white American Army Colonel reprimanded the waitress for making him wait until she served the group. He stated very loudly that were he came from, Niggers weren't allowed in the same place with whites. The manager very quickly replied that he was not in America now and that the nurses were guests. Therefore, he could return to the ferry without any service.

On weekends, all shops closed and people went to relax and frolic on the beaches. One Sunday, Hathaway and her buddies went to the beach. They had hemmed slacks to wear as swim shorts. Hathaway walked out into the ocean until the water was up to her neck, then she began to make swim like strokes to fool the observers. All of a sudden, a big wave knocked her over. The guards came to her rescue and when they picked her up, was she ever embarrassed!!!, because sand had collected in the hem of the pants and she looked like a hippopotamus being dragged from the sea. People on the beach sat up laughing and said, "What is that?" Never again would she try to show off in the water. Sharks were known to come into the beach area. Many Australians had been washed away. Prime Minister Holt was never found.

Another interesting feature in Australia was to see the pedestrians walk crisscross corners to cross the streets when the lights changed. Years later Hathaway witnessed this same pattern when she attended a Health Care Analysis for the state conference in Denver, Colorado. Flowers were all over the streets, banks of flowers along the railroad tracks from city to city. When Hathaway had geography in school, she never dreamed that one day she would visit the continent that was shaped upside down, the opposite of the United States' shape.

The Pittsburgh Courier paper printed articles and pictures of the Negro Army Nurses in Australia. They rode horseback which was the first time Hathaway had ever been on a horse. She had fears of horses when she had to ride in Mollie's buggy during her childhood days in Illinois. One buddy was given a horse that was blind and when she began to fall off, she caught onto the horse's mane and her behind went up into mid air - the group cracked up laughing. Hathaway immediately got off her horse - never again!

They cycled all over the areas. Hathaway again thanked Bruce for teaching her how to ride a bicycle in her young days.

The group never had a dull moment as they waited for their hospital to be completed in the jungles of New Guinea. They had to do KP assignment for all of the nurses but when it cam time for meals, the Negro nurses all had to eat at one table away from the white nurses. They were housed in one barracks separate from the others. They were scheduled officers of the day on a rotation basis in the office. The minute they were free of duty, Hathaway and her buddies took the train into the city. Hathaway was having too much fun to worry about the Army's segregation actions. In fact, all her life she had been too busy doing her own thing to be intimidated by segregation.

The Pittsburgh Courier circulated pictures and stories of the fifteen Negro Army Nurses in Australia. When the paper reached Southern Illinois, the people were overwhelmed and excited. To think the one person they had ridiculed and had made derogatory statements that she would never be anything but have a house full of bastards like her mama, had put their town on the map, worldwide news, one of their very own, Hathaway!! The town people wrote a letter of appreciation to Elizabeth and asked that she send it to Hathaway with a request to send them a message to be read at the next town meeting. Hathaway received the letter. On the back of it she wrote, "Kiss my A--" and returned it to her mother. Elizabeth never showed the answer, she was too ashamed. She had hoped that her daughter had changed in her attitudes toward these people. No way, Jose!!

One week after Hathaway had left for the South Pacific, Lt. Templeton received Orders for the European area. Eighteen days at sea, then moving from Sydney to Brisbane, letters were very late in reaching Hathaway. Although Hathaway had participated in and had enjoyed all of the exciting activities in Australia, she constantly thought of Templeton. She missed him and longed for their romantic nights in each other's arms, just the reminiscent of those moments sent chills through her body. If only he were here with her. They were so close to being married. When there were periods of no mail from Lt. Templeton, Hathaway would become impossible to live with. Her buddies told her that she was horrible.

The nurses received a message that the ship carrying the hospital unit to New Guinea had been wrecked on the reefs in the Coral Sea. This mishap caused a delay in their arrival consequently, it would be another month before the completion of the hospital. Of course that meant the nurses would have to spend Christmas in Brisbane. Excitement of the new experience in Australia had begun to decrease. The nurses were ready for duty.

The color barrier was forgotten during the holiday festivities. The black and white nurses together sang carols on the camp grounds and at the Army Chapel. Years later at the University of Minnesota, Hathaway and one of the white nurses talked about their participation in this same event, but at the time because of segregation, they did not know each other. Later they were roommates at the university.

After December, Hathaway and comrades were alerted to proceed by ship to their newly built hospital with a bed capacity of two hundred and fifty in the jungles of New Guinea. The medics of the hospital had built the hospital with prefabricated material from Australia. Not a nail was used.

Everyone was happy to finally see each other after such a long period of separation. Other troops in the area heard that fifteen Black Army Nurses had arrived to staff the new hospital. They had no idea Black Nurses had been recruited into the service. In order to show their appreciation that someone cared enough to come to give them medical aid, they gave a welcoming party for the nurses. Too, they had not seen an American Black female for many months and they were anxious to find out if any of the nurses were from their home town or state. They had a delicious dinner followed by a fabulous stage show. Those who acted as chorus girls, had mops on their heads for hair. It was an enjoyable evening.

The natives were interesting; Black Aborigines. They lived in thatch type shelter, slept on beautifully woven designed and colorful straw mats (at one time the same type mats used in the rich American people's homes during summer months), they worked in the coconut groves on the island. The men wore only "g" strings, no shoes (toes spread out like eagle toes), hair was matted with all colors streaking through from the use of turpentine they had obtained from ships. They spoke no English, only a gibberish type sound; their teeth were black from the betel nut obtained from the trees they chewed that gave the same effects as alcohol.

The women wore grass skirts only and never removed the skirt, but when a child was born, a new one was placed over the old one; this cycle continued and one underneath would rot away. They never bathed. The nearest they came in touch with water was when the baby was born by the shoreline to wash the new born. Their hair was same as the men; toes spread out the same.

The food consisted of coconuts and fish. The men did the diving for fish. Cooking took place in large black pots for some and others used only an open fire with cross bars. There were very old banty roosters running around the yards. (The nurses cooked one that never became edible).

Since the natives had many types of contagious tropical diseases, their quarters and close contact were off limits to the Army personnel. However, when special tours in certain areas were allowed and one obtained any of the natives' grass mats or skirts, the articles would have to be auto claved before being shipped to America. One could observe every type of tropical disease in the world.

The men protected their wives from any intrusions. They had the boomerang that could be used for fighting and hunting. The average life span of the natives was thirty-two years. There was a tropical disease hospital provided for the natives under the supervision of the Australian government. Doctors came every six months and in the interim natives who had been trained, gave what little care the ill received.

Barbara Hutton and Errol Flynn each owned villas on islands nearby that were accessible only by boat. Head hunters inhabited many of the islands. A plane carrying a group from Broad-

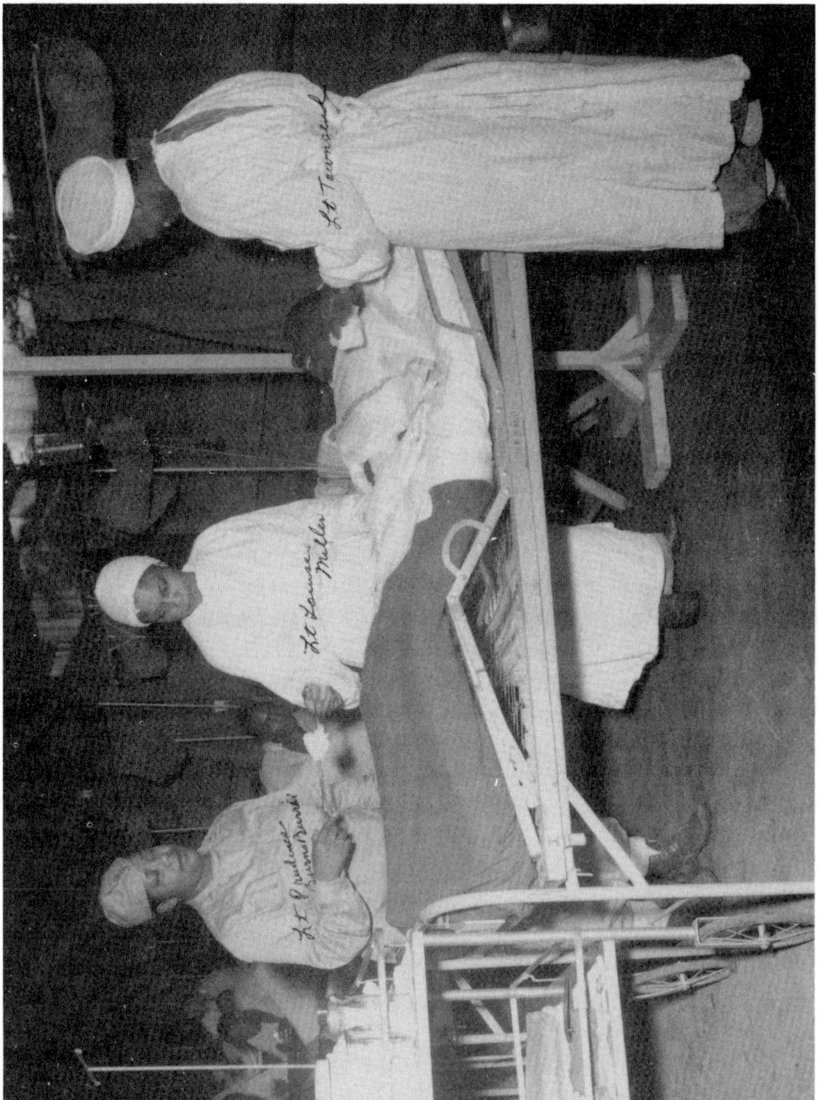

Milnea Bay, New Guinea, 1943

way enroute to entertain the troops crashed into one of the mountains and all aboard were supposed to have perished. The gossip was that the Japs shot it down in an area where head hunters lived, that the pilot apparently wanted to show the group the head hunters area and flew too close. How would anyone know this since no one survived? The weather was very hot and it rained almost daily. The rain created swamp areas that were infested with anopheles mosquitoes that transmitted the malaria. The female mosquito did her damage after six p.m. by biting a person on the neck and wrist. These islands had the highest rate of deadly types of malaria in the world. A nationally known epidemiologist from America came to the islands and conducted workshops for the hospital staff.

Atabrane was given as a protective and suppressive measure. The medication turned the pigment yellow or dark green skin. Hathaway would not take the medicine because she had obtained an immunity when she had the disease during her childhood. At the time it stunned the doctor because malaria was not supposed to be found in a Northern City. Her co-workers never knew but of course her dear friend, Lt. L.H. knew.

Lt. L.H. was the Adjutant of the hospital. He was like a brother to Hathaway and continued to look after her as he had promised Lt. Templeton. He tried to keep her out of trouble because she would speak out on any issue that she disapproved. Once she asked an inspecting general to court-martial one of the captains. After a lengthy discussion, she settled for a reprimand and if he crossed her again, then a court-martial. Another time, she challenged the commanding officer in a troop meeting. Later he and Lt. LH brought a colonel from the surgeon general's office to her ward. During their inspection, they knew her ward would be impressive. The colonel said, "Oh, someone must have told you that I was coming because everything is so neat and clean." Hathaway snapped to attention and said, "Sir! I do not clean for visitors. I clean for myself and my ward is always clean." He, her commanding officer and Lt. LH all turned red and immediately left her ward. Her commanding officer later returned and told Hathaway that she would challenge the devil. She asked him why hadn't he told the General that the ward was well run at all times. Apparently he thought so because he used her ward for all visitors.

Mail during wartime is something for the birds. Hathaway lived each day for letters from Lt. Templeton. Occasionally weeks went by without a word. Loneliness began to develop in spite of Lt. LH's companionship. Soldiers from her home town saw to her receiving pounds of ice daily, fresh fish, beer, etc. Her Army type round icebox had to be hidden during inspection days.

The Commanding Officer of the hospital apparently developed a special interest in Hathaway. She was given an assignment to fly with an Australian pilot to escort patients to Fenchaven Island for evacuation to the United States. This was Hathaway's first time in her life on a plane.

She told Lt. LH that she needed diapers for the trip. Pampers had not become known at that time. The pilot taught her how to help him with the controls. On their return to her unit, the pilot asked if she wanted to fly over the head hunter's area where the plane went down with the Broadway show people? It was storming and she had to keep the windshield wipers going plus help with other controls. Hathaway told him that he bloody well knew that she was not interested in the head hunters' place or anything else other than to get the plane back to her station. He cracked up laughing and teased her that the Americans had learned the word "Bloody." On this trip Hathaway had had an opportunity to see some of the officers of the 93rd Division whom she had met at Fort Huachuca in Arizona.

The Commanding Officer of the 1311 Engineer's Corps contacted the hospital commanding officer for a teacher to develop a program of basic principles and demonstrations on how to develop and operate a dispensary for his troops. Hathaway was given the assignment. She developed a program whereby she used all of the fourteen nurses to lecture in their expertise. This way she maintained a healthy friendly relationship with her comrades. The soldiers in the class really liked her. They brought her gallons of coke syrup, fish, ice, beer, candy and whatever they thought she would like. She tried to tell those who were doing poorly in the classes that the gifts were not going to get them a passing grade. They stated they did not care whether they passed on or not, that they would continue to bring gifts because they liked her as a nice person. Those who did not listen, she flunked out, exactly as she had done her students in her Public Health classes. One of soldiers did exceptionally well in the class. Every week, whiskey in loaves of bread came to him from relatives and he gave fifths to Hathaway. She in turn shared it with her buddies since she didn't drink. She rationed three glasses of the whiskey a day to her friend Lt. LH. Later he laughed about it because he was officer of supplies and could have all of the whiskey he wanted.

In Hathaway's ward was a Marine. When he was discharged, he asked her if she had a wish for any kind of food from the ship. Hathaway told him that she was sick of Spam cooked all kinds of ways day in and day out. He went back to his company and obtained permission to bring a crate of steaks to her. Since Lt. LH was the Mess Hall Officer, Hathaway asked him to have the staff cook the steaks and serve them to the whole unit, officers and enlisted personnel alike.

Hathaway and Lt. LH were beginning to become very close. She kept hers and his khakis starched and ironed as if a commercial laundry was in the area. The patients on her ward could watch for the Lt., as he walked from his quarters to his office and they would make remarks about his style of walking in his ironed khakis. Then the rain would come and he would continue to walk in the rain. She would become so angry with him for letting the rain damage her hard work of ironing. In the evenings she would darn her white silk long sleeved blouse, ironed khakis and pants legs draped in white socks turned down over her combat boots. Since she was kinda plump she had her Army khakis tailor-made instead of wearing the issued type that was flimsy and horrible looking on a fat person. She and the Lt. would attend the outdoor movies in the rain as they sat under their ponchos. Later she would prepare a night snack from exotic foods sent from Wanamakers Store in Pennsylvania. She made a tablecloth and napkins from one of the sheets. (Hathaway still has the glass used for the rationed whiskey and improvised table linen used over forty years ago.)

During her night duty assignments, the Lt. would come and sit throughout the night. They shared intimate secrets in their lives. She told him all about her episodes from high school, nurses' training, love affairs before enlistment and the present with Lt. Templeton. Anxiety for Lt. Templeton was beginning to take the back burner. Something about Lt. LH had begun to bother her; was she falling in love with him? Or was he falling in love with her?

Officers in another area heard about the hospital nurses being in a area not too far from them. On weekends they would come over to visit. One of the officers took a liking to Hathaway. Lt. LH did not think she should see him. The next weekend when they came to the hospital, Lt. LH told the officer that Hathaway had a seriously ill patient on her unit, therefore she would not come up to the mess hall that night so he might as well go back to camp. Lt. LH had her supper brought to the ward. She was surprised when the soldier brought the supper and stated that Lt. LH had told him to bring her the supper. She had planned to see the visiting officers. Later, the supervisor came to the ward and wanted to know who and when had a patient become seriously ill. Hathaway thought "what's with Lt. LH?" She did not have a seriously ill patient.

One of the unit doctors became critically ill with a ruptured appendix and had to be brought back to life while on the operating table. Hathaway was assigned to special him around the clock. That type of assignment curtailed her night session with Lt. LH. He told her that he would be glad when they could resume their sessions together. Ironically, she also had the same feeling. After a month, the doctor no longer needed special care.

Lt. LH asked Hathaway for a date, not a friendship type as they had going. He kissed her goodnight just as the two were leaving her unit. She thought about the kiss and its effect on her. He had the same technique at Lt. Templeton. She couldn't decide which one was more handsome than the other. Lt. LH was admired by several of the nurses. Hathaway thought that he was interested in one of her close buddies. The buddy was very cute, well shaped, small and witty. She said, "No, I am not interested in Lt. LH." Another one tried to nail him but he wasn't interested in her. The husband of Hathaway's grade school classmate whom she had visited and driven their car at the Fort in

Arizona, was one of the doctors in the unit. He knew Lt. Templeton and began to tease Hathaway that it looked as if she would have to make a choice between two handsome officers.

Gradually the relationship of big brother and protective actions faded only to be replaced by a very romantic affair. He had not been a lay reader in the church as Lt. Templeton, although he should have been, because he too had a deep melodious smooth voice. The nurses loved to talk with him.

There had been a movie about the activities of the white Army nurses and a special section on how they had planned an exciting and happy Christmas holiday. Some had obtained beautiful lace black nightgowns that they wore for evening dresses to the party in their barracks. Hathaway wrote Ms. Chandler for a black nightgown. Ms. Chandler found a gorgeous one in St. Louis. Hathaway modeled the gown for Lt. LH. He loved it.

Lt. LH and Hathaway spent many romantic hours together whenever possible. Areas to be alone in the jungles were very limited. Spooning had to take place in Army motor vehicles only as one rode around the grounds. Lt. LH was Officer of Transportation, therefore it was not too much of a problem. Hathaway shall never in her life forget one romantic evening. Her nurses' training days of full sessions with her peers suddenly flashed back. Now she knew what the classmates meant when she had asked "if they had had their bell rung." Her schoolmate buddy in the barracks cracked up when Hathaway confronted her. Hathaway was serious because she had thought that she had experienced a heart attack!

Hathaway sent a letter to Lt. Templeton to tell him that she was breaking her engagement because she and Lt. LH were planning to get married. She asked that he forgive her. Within two weeks a letter came from the Red Cross to inform her that Lt. Templeton had been critically wounded in combat, that when he was given her letter, he blacked out again. Since she was listed as one of his beneficiaries, please wait at least another week before making contact again and keep in touch with the Red Cross.

The Commanding Officer changed the administrative officer in the nursing department. The chief nurse was removed and Lt.

Birt became the new chief nurse with Lt. Hathaway as the assistant chief nurse. In the meeting concerning these changes, Hathaway told the commanding officer that if he made her assistant just to get her support in situations that she did not endorse, then he had better appoint someone else. The Commanding Officer stated that he wanted two chiefs to develop a well-run chief nurse program. The Commanding Officer of the 1311 Engineer corps sent a letter of commendation and thanks to Hathaway and her commanding officer for the well conducted classes for his troops. Was there anything he could do for her? Yes! She asked that he arrange for the nurses to visit the Tropical Disease Hospital for the natives. She had heard they had every kind of tropical disease in the world.

The observation trip was arranged and when it came time to go, Hathaway had to attend a meeting. All of the other nurses went and reported back that the hospital was managed by an Australian attendant. The doctor came every six months. The beds were stone slabs with shredded pieces of blankets for cover. They saw patients with elephantiasis, yaws, skin leprosy and various types of malaria.

Hathaway and Lt. LH began to talk of marriage. He wrote his mother to purchase an engagement ring and wedding band. Elizabeth was stunned because Lt. Templeton had visited her before he was sent to the European theater of war. Well, it was left up to her to plan her own life. Hathaway and Lt. LH decided to purchase their home in order to have their own place when they returned to the states. He again contacted his mother in Michigan to have a real estate company send pictures of houses for sale. They made their choice and each matched dollars necessary to close the deal. Lt. LH wanted the marriage to take place in the states. Hathaway wanted to have a military wedding in the South Pacific. Well, at least they had a home to begin their life together.

Orders came for the unit to move. The staff had to attend Spanish classes in preparation for assignment in the Philippines. Packing and closing up the hospital was a chore and headache. The final move was to proceed to the Philippines. All troops were to meet General MacArthur for the invasion of Japan.

Manila was in shambles. People were homeless; orphaned children roamed the streets hungry. They would dig into the Army garbage pails for food. General Wainright, troops, nurses and Phillippinos were freed after having been held captive for months in the University of Santa Thomas. Many could not stand because they had been made to squat for months. They were emaciated and looked horrible. Snipers ran into the hills and at night they would come back and kill the soldiers. Orders were issued to not travel alone and without weapons. One male black civilian who had lived in the Philippines for years witnessed the Jap soldiers bayonet his baby. They were supposed to have killed the babies for food. They had killed and eaten all the cats and dogs. Another black man from the Caribbean lived quite well in a villa and was into politics. When he heard about the Black Army Hospital Unit being in the area, he had a formal dinner party. Later he was tried as a collaborator with the enemy. The article appeared in Time magazine. He was acquitted of the accusations.

Just as they had done in Australia, Hathaway and her buddies explored the city. They got to know many Philippino families. They adopted one of the little orphaned girl, saw to her having clothes and food. All of the nurses, Black and White, just as they had done in Australia, had to share quarters in the St. Joseph Academy. Once again they had to do KP and rotate as officer of the day in the office.

During one of Hathaway's assignments as officer of the day, a call came. The male officer stated he was calling for a date to accompany him to the officer's club for formal dinner and dance scheduled for Friday night. Before she could give him any information, he said, "What about your being my date; your voice is lovely, so you must be a lovely officer." Hathaway asked if he knew about the hospital stationed in the South Pacific and gave him the number of her hospital unit. He stated that of courses he knew the unit; Liar! When she told him that the unit was of all Negroes and she was a Negro Army nurse, he stated that she was pulling his leg because her use of English and voice were not that of a Negro. Her answer to him was that we as a race have people who know how to speak with usage of correct English and have excellent speaking voices. He ended the long drawn out hassle by saying, "I don't give a damn if you are a Negro, will you be my date?" Hathaway told him OK, she would accompany him to the dance.

Lt. LH visited Hathaway every night. She told him about the incident. That Friday, the white officer came dressed in full formal uniform. With him was a tall Texas officer.

One of the white nurses was officer of the day and when she came back in the quarters to tell Hathaway that she had visitors in the lounge, she said, "How in the hell can you have two handsome white officers calling when I can't even get one?" She thought Lt. LH was also white. The white officers did not act surprised when he actually saw that Hathaway really was a Negro. He asked her if she were ready; that he was from California and would love for her to give him the honor. His comrade asked him if he were crazy. He said. "Let's get the hell out of here." Hathaway introduced the California officer to Lt. LH. The two recognized each other as having trained together at Camp Pickett, consequently they had a long bull session. He had been Lt. LH's professor and Lt. LH had been listed as white! Lt. LH had them change it immediately to Negro.

Hathaway and her buddies enrolled in a typing class there in the Academy. When classes ended, they hit the streets to continue to explore the city. They met many people. One family had relatives in Pennsylvania; another one's husband was one of the secretaries for President Osmena of the Philippines. This family's home had not been destroyed. It was similar to a villa. The interior was gorgeously furnished with an exotic Spanish type motif. The Army had given Spanish classes to the troops before they left for this assignment but when they arrived in Manila, the people spoke a language called Tagalog. The Philippines stated that it was a combination of Spanish and their local dialect. The nurses managed to communicate. They shopped around town. Hathaway began to buy the beautiful hand made linens for her trousseau. The Australian friends sent packages of cookies, cheese and canned meats for snacks to Hathaway and a couple of her buddies all the time they were in the jungles. When one of the families learned of her engagement to Lt. LH, they sent a beautiful set of forks with pearl handled knives, soup spoons, and Australian teakwood napkin rings. (As of today, Hathaway has every article obtained at that time.)

Suddenly the bombing of Hiroshima ended the hostilities, but not before a group of medicals arrived. In the group was Doctor CM, Hathaway's ex-lover when she was a Public Health Nurse in the Midwest City. He asked the officers where were the nurses' quarters in the island because he wanted to visit one of the nurses. He was told to ask Lt. LH if he could go with him because he went every night to the nurses's quarters. Ironically, neither one discussed whom he was to visit. When they arrived at the nurses' quarters, Hathaway went through the same experience as of last week. The white officer of the day asked Hathaway how did she rate a date with two officers who looked like twins and the most handsome officers she had ever seen in the area? Hathaway told her that she dated only handsome men. She knew LH was coming but who was the other officer? She knew that both Lt. LH and Lt. Templeton were handsome but one was brown and the other mulatto. Who was this second officer?

Was Hathaway in for a big surprise? The second officer was Captain CM. He gave her a big hug and kisses. Lt. LH stood looking. When she finally became free of CM's tight embrace, she attempted to introduce the two. They told her that they had met and ridden in together. Hathaway was happy to see him and he tried to bring her up to date on events since they had left Huachuca. His wife (that he, Hathaway and Hubert had had the confrontation with in a movie) and also his mother had died. After having sat between the two until an opportune time, Hathaway asked if they had told each other whom he was coming to visit? They said, "No." Hathaway told Captain CM that she and Lt. LH were engaged. He said, "I am sorry, so I shall leave." When Hathaway walked him to the door, he asked if she'd have lunch with him just for pleasure. "Sorry, but I refuse to play the same game twice?" He said, "It's no game this time; I wish I had married you in the beginning." Hathaway said, "Too late," goodbye. When she told Lt. LH, he only smiled.

All along, LH was holding out for a Stateside wedding. Hathaway wanted a military wedding to take place before re-

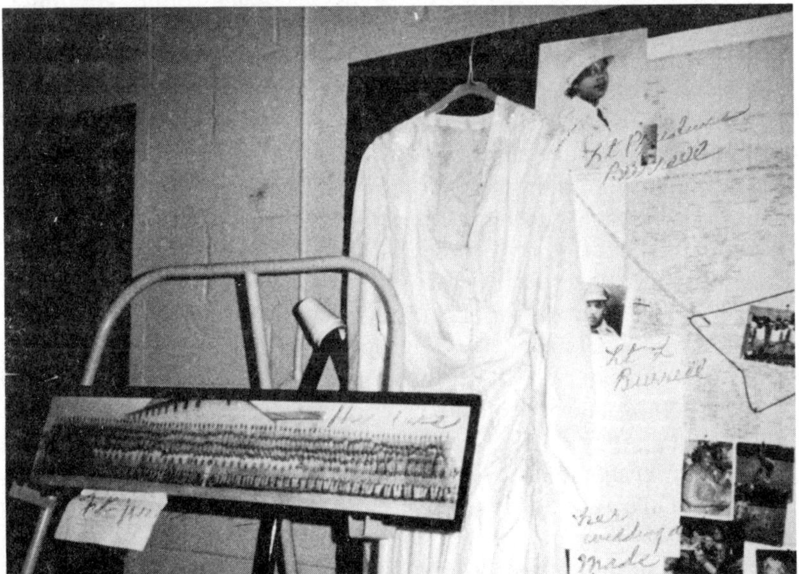

Marriage 1945—Manila, Philippines
Dress made from parachute.

turning to the states. The nurses had to wear pants, high top boot-type shoes, hair rolled in rat-called cloth, etc. She felt it would be better to nab this man now before they returned State-side where the glamorous gals with access to all of the beauty aids had remained. Well, after Captain CM's visit, Hathaway got her wish.

The very next day, Lt. LH came with the twenty-five pages of forms the Army required to be filled in for permission to be married. Hathaway was familiar with the forms since she and Lt. Templeton had to go through the same procedure which usually took at least a month for the Red Cross to process. Lt. LH had taken care of the time element. The two had to hand carry the forms to each office for signature. By the end of the day, they obtained permission, but had only a week before the nurses would leave for the states.

The day was Monday, so they set the wedding date for Wednesday, October 17, 1945. Wheels began turning! All of her comrades pitched in to help; one of the Red Cross workers sketched her wedding dress - slenderizing wraparound skirt, v-neckline bodice, long sleeves. Philippine friends found a dress-maker who copied the sketch to a "T." She used parachute material, sewed tiny pearl buttons on all folds in the skirt and on the panels extending from the shoulders and looped at the waist before buttoning in the back. Hathaway was kept awake all night with black coffee for fittings. In the meantime her comrade took a hospital sheet to make the underslip.

Since the rings from his mother had not arrived, they bought gold wedding bands with "Philippines 1945" engraved at the cost of 50 cents per ring (that gold has held up for 40 years. Hathaway lost hers in later years in San Francisco in 1960.) They left the trinket shop and headed for the Filipino Court House to obtain their marriage license. The jeep they were riding in broke down. The office was to close at five o'clock and time was running out. Hathaway got out of the jeep and stood by the side of the road to thumb a ride. Along came a deuce and half ton Army truck filled with black soldiers. Whey they saw her, they stopped, began to scream, yell and salute. They stated they would take her any place she wished. One should have seen their faces when Lt. LH came up into the road. They helped Hathaway up into the truck. She actually needed a ladder, so one soldier pulled while another pushed her behind up. Everyone cracked up, but the soldiers got them to the office and offered congratulations. They were invited to the wedding reception.

The Filipino social secretary to President Osmena and his wife let Hathaway use her Mestiza Wedding Veil which had been used for three generations. The wedding reception was held in their home and the couple rented an apartment within their villa for the honeymoon.

Lt. LH was an Episcopalian. The double ring wedding took place in the Navy's CB Chapel with Father Stairs officiating. Others in the wedding were their comrades. The pharmacist was best man. Chief Nurse Lt. Birt was matron of honor. Captain R.B. Fleming gave Hathaway away (he was the night superintendent of the hospital where Hathaway had trained.) Her commanding officer really didn't like it; he wanted to give her away. Sandy sang "Because." The Famous Larry Keyes known as 88 keys was touring the Far East. His pianist repertoire and fascinatingly familiar and new interpretations kept the mood lively during the entire evening. The Pittsburgh Courier printed a lengthy story of the wedding.

Captain Flemings used his movie camera to take many pictures of the wedding. The most outstanding one was of the Lt. faking his carrying Hathaway over the threshold into their apartment. Everyone teased him by saying if he had actually taken her up into his arms with all her weight, he would have never in a lifetime been able to consummate the marriage. Captain Flemings sent the movie to his wife who in turn showed it at one of the Colored graduate nurses' association meetings. He would not release it to Hathaway to have copies made. There were other Army activities on the film and he felt if he let it go, he would never see it again. Captain Flemings is now deceased and no one knows where to find the film. Many years later Hathaway teasingly asked LH if he remembered his remark after the wedding. He said, "No." He had said, "Finally all mine!"

The Navato family served the couple a Filipino breakfast which consisted of raw fish, tiny cocktail shrimp, rice, their special kind of bread, champagne and wine. Hathaway could not eat raw fish.

One week after the marriage, Hathaway and the nurses left by ship for the states. This time she had to rough it without Lt. LH's reassurance and help if she had to abandon the ship. Finally they docked at the Port of Tacoma, Washington. Did they ever create a stare in the downtown shopping center. One young white girl introduced herself to Hathaway and told her that she too was a nurse there in Tacoma and was out on maternity leave.

The nurses traveled by train to a camp in Iowa. There was utter chaos with the railroad personnel. They were confronted with the need for many trains to transport all of the troops that seemed to have crowded all stations, wanting to hurry home now that the hostilities had ended. The lines were crowded with all kinds of dilapidated trains. The nurses' train was sidetracked in many states. Either it had to wait for other trains to pass or to correct some mechanical problem. Something good comes out of something bad every time. The stops in various states gave Hathaway an opportunity to purchase a lot of knickknacks, mementos and articles necessary for a kitchen in her home.

They finally arrived at a Fort in Iowa for discharge. They were very angry for being sent to the Fort because it was a Fort for the WAC. People were confused about the difference of the two Corps. Now they were sent here for discharges. Once Hathaway was cleared, she took a train to St. Louis, did some shopping, bought a turkey for Elizabeth's Thanksgiving dinner, then took a bus to Southern Illinois.

One should have heard the people who happened to be near the bus station when Hathaway stepped off the bus. She walked very proudly with a conceited grin on her face. Elizabeth began to cry when Hathaway entered the house. For once, they gave each other a big kiss and hug. Later in the day, Hathaway's classmate, who had ignored her every Xmas at party time in her home, came to the house. She stated that a group of citizens were so proud of her Army record and that she was the only female officer from the area, therefore they would like for her to be the guest at a luncheon celebration to express their appreciation.

Hathaway told her that she did not want anything from the

people in this town who had ridiculed her most of her life, that when she, the classmate, used to have a Xmas yearly party and invite all of the girls except her because she did not have proper clothing, she used to cry when she was isolated, shunned and ridiculed. Well, she would cry no more; that she did not go to college to be accepted by people. Her priorities were to improve her life, help her mother to a better way of life, therefore tell them to take their luncheon and stick it up!

When she had gone, Elizabeth admonished Hathaway, stated she had thought there would be a change in her attitude, but, No! There never would be in a lifetime. Hathaway told her, No, she had never been a hypocrite. If she didn't like a person, he or she knew it because she had never pretended an attitude with a person, either she liked them or not; that included relatives also. Too, so many of the people in this town had been unforgiveably mean to her during her growing-up life.

Ms. Chandler had Hathaway visit the elementary classrooms. The students were elated and asked many types of questions that showed they knew social studies very well which at that time was divided into individual subjects. Later in years, some of those students, now adults, remember Hathaway's visit to their classrooms. Some became registered nurses, and went in the Armed Forces.

Genuine friends had Hathaway model her wedding gown. They congratulated and wished her well. They were so proud of her. When they saw LH's picture, they remarked that he and Lt. Templeton were two handsome men and asked how LH had wooed her from Lt. Templeton. A few people had seen Lt. Templeton when he visited Elizabeth.

Hathaway asked Elizabeth to accompany her to the city in Michigan where she and LH had bought their home while they were stationed in New Guinea. She was quite anxious to see their house. Elizabeth agreed to accompany her providing she returned home by December in order to prepare Xmas for her young grandson, Eddie. With Hathaway's promise to have her back just before Xmas, they, Hathaway, Elizabeth and her granddaughter took the train for Michigan. Hathaway was happy to have Elizabeth and her granddaughter with her and for once there seemed to be a bondage of love. Hathaway, for over six months while in the jungles, would, for no reason, have crying spells and period of depression.

When they arrived in the Michigan station, awaiting them were LH's mother and aunt. Soldiers were cheering and saluting Hathaway. Civilians came over to shake hands and thank her for serving her country. The aunt of LH gave Hathaway a big hug and kiss. His mother stood aside and just stared. Hathaway whispered to Elizabeth and said, "I see I am in for hell, but I shall deal with it, believe me." Elizabeth said, "Please! Be nice."

The house was a small five-room frame that had excellent potentials to become a beautiful cozy home. Once Hathaway had gotten over the obstacles and rid of a couple of relatives who had moved in with LH's mother and just refused to move, she began to take stock of the changes and repairs needed in order to make it a beautiful home.

The first priority was to remove the one and only gas heater. Hathaway had just come from a warm climate into ice, snow and extremely cold weather. It was more than she could tolerate. Naturally with the snow knee deep, the installation of a furnace cost a fortune. Wallpaper inches thick had to be steamed off and replaced with pastel shades of paint. Three to four linoleums had to be removed and the floors sanded down to beautiful wood when highly polished and buffed. The bathroom walls and floor were tiled. Furniture Hathaway had in her apartment in the Midwest has been shipped to her brother who had been in the service and lived in this city. He in turn had the furniture moved to her new house. A beautiful bar cabinet was purchased and completely stocked for LH's arrival. Some remodeling was started on the attic to make it into a recreation room. Everything was now in order and waiting for LH to arrive from the Philippines.

The snow was exceptionally deep, therefore Hathaway begged Elizabeth to wait for the weather to subside somewhat, but NO! She was adamant and determined to return to Southern Illinois for Christmas. She felt her grandson would not have a good Christmas if she were not there to purchase his gifts. Hathaway knew that the trip would be horrible, for they had experienced the ordeal coming to Michigan. In order to move the troops, the railroad companies used coaches badly in need of repairs, cold, windows broken etc. Elizabeth was in one of these coaches that was cold and drafty with broken windows. She caught a cold that developed into pneumonia.

Mrs. Chandler came to visit for the holidays. Two weeks after Elizabeth had gone home, a telegram came from one of Hathaway's brothers. It read: "Please come immediately. Elizabeth is sick." Hathaway told Mrs. Chandler that Elizabeth was dying because the sad feeling of depression she had been encountering for six months had suddenly disappeared; she had strange feelings of retrospect that on several occasions during Elizabeth's visit, she would look up and find Elizabeth staring at her. Hathaway shared all of this with Mrs. Chandler as they took the train back to Southern Illinois. She told her that Elizabeth was dying. Mrs. Chandler said, "No, the telegram had stated that she was ill."

The minute Hathaway saw Elizabeth and heard her breathing, she knew the end was near. Elizabeth called, "Hathaway," then pointed to her throat. There was Cheyen-Stokes respiration. Hathaway had her brother to call a doctor who was not the family doctor and had not ordered any antibiotics. In the meantime, Hathaway bathed and dressed Elizabeth for a trip to the hospital. She had gone to her doctor of the family and her close friend only to learn that he was out of town. She practically ordered the housekeeper to call long distance to tell him that Hathaway needed him immediately. Another friend of Hathaway's had a business ten miles away in the city where the hospital was located. He dropped everything and drove his ambulance through sleet and snow to take Elizabeth to the hospital.

The hospital was Catholic and segregated. They had to take Elizabeth to the back entrance and through the male ward to the female side. Hathaway's friend, before he left, gave her one hundred dollars in the event she needed it for any type of treatment that must be paid for in advance. The hospital doctor was white and in U.S. Army uniform, so was Hathaway. When she said that she was an Army Nurse he began immediately giving the staff orders as he and Hathaway worked on her mother. For supper, Hathaway fed her some clear broth. Later that evening, December 25, 1945, Elizabeth passed. Another son, Lenny, was enroute home from the war. LH had not gotten home either, therefore, he and Elizabeth never met.

To handle all of the business details for Elizabeth's funeral was quite an ordeal for Hathaway. She met all kinds of opposition from her siblings. They wanted to bring the body home for the "wake" (now called Family Hour) instead of viewing the body at the mortuary. When Hathaway protested, they began to ridicule her and told her that she felt she was better than they were; to hell with her educated ideas. Just before Elizabeth's body was brought home, Hathaway rushed home in order to check last minute details. Luckily that she did, because the brothers and friends were in the middle of the floor drinking booze. She reprimanded them and they stated a scripture in the Bible... "When there is death, one should be merry." Hathaway told one cantankerous brother that if he did not settle down there would be two funerals because she would knock his brains out with one of the flat irons.

Hathaway went to the bank to clear up the account and learned that while Elizabeth was with her in Michigan, one of her sons forged her signature and withdrew all of the savings of six-hundred dollars. This savings was the Army money Lenny had sent home. Elizabeth knew he would ask for it when he returned so, instead of using it, she used the Army allotment Hathaway had sent to her every month.

Hathaway obtained an Administrator for Elizabeth's estate. He drew up a statement for restitution of the money and had the son and wife to sign. They were to pay a sum each month. In this small town, gossip on everyone's actions went on daily. Everyone, even the bank manger, who had grown up there and worked in his father's store, knew that Elizabeth, had gone with Hathaway to visit and help her get her new house in order. He should have known better than to honor the withdrawal slip. Years later, the manager went to prison for embezzlement.

When Lenny arrived, the family told him that Hathaway had taken his six-hundred dollars Elizabeth had in the bank for him. She had taken it to remodel her new home in Michigan. Hathaway was shocked. Lenny angrily wrote Hathaway to at least send him enough money to buy civilian clothes. The Administrator had told him what had happened to his money and showed him the signed document by his brother. Lenny didn't believe it.

The brother has never paid Lenny the money and to date Hathaway believes Lenny thinks she took his money. Years later he used money he had gotten from Hathaway to purchase a radio as a gift. He never paid back the money and told her she owed him something.

It took years for Hathaway to overcome the hurt and attacks from her siblings. After all, she had worked through the years to help Elizabeth support these children. She had picked beans, peaches, strawberries, chopped corn, worked in a delicatessen and private homes for teachers. Sometimes they could not eat until Hathaway came in from work with food. All of these things flashed back through Hathaway's mind as she attempted to cope with Elizabeth's death and the sibling harassment.

A month later Hathaway's husband LH was finally discharged. It was good to have him home to help her through the episodes of depression. Life took on a healthier meaning. She could cope with anything as long as she had LH's encouragement.

LH was quite pleased with the house. He especially liked his Christmas present: a portable cabinet type bar stocked with his favorite liquors. Since he and Hathaway had spent fourteen months in the jungles of the South Pacific during WW II, Hathaway had the refrigerator stocked with all kinds of fresh vegetables and meats and the walk-in pantry stocked with canned goods.

They acted like newlyweds... "truly two love birds" from the dining room to the bedroom. At three or four A.M., Hathaway would cook a full course meal, even blackberry cobblers and they would eat as if they were starved and there would be no tomorrow.

The two began to settle in and make plans for the future. LH enrolled in an accounting program and worked part time with an insurance agency. Hathaway began working with the Visiting Nurses Association. The same principles of segregation existed here as when she was a Visiting Nurse in the Midwest town in

Missouri. Black nurses assigned to black families and whites to white only. The staff was integrated but no blacks were supervisors except the office where Hathaway was assigned. Two black supervisors managed the office.

Hathaway had been working just about two months when Mrs. Chandler became ill and wanted her to accompany her to Mayo Clinic. Immediately Hathaway went to the Director and told her the reason she must resign because she had not worked long enough for time off. The Director told her that she would not accept the resignation, to take all the time she needed, that her job would be waiting, that she had been hired in the beginning because of excellent recommendations and such a pleasant interview.

When Hathaway returned to her job, one of the supervisors began to harass her. She would give Hathaway the complicated cases in other nurses' areas instead of her own assigned district; would make snide remarks about her knowing so much about public health and perhaps Hathaway would like to be a supervisor. This supervisor would chew and pop gum all during office hours so that one could hardly concentrate when writing reports.

Hathaway was becoming established in the city and did not wish to make waves. She was getting vibes from all directions, on the job and at home. By the same token she had begun to meet very friendly people. In one of the grocery stores near her office, she met a lovely lady who introduced her to club members at the Lucy Thruman Y., the pharmacist, who was best man at their wedding, and family lived near her office. Also their house became Grand Central Station when ex-Army nurses and doctors who had either interned or worked with her learned that she and LH had moved into the city. Army buddies of hers and LH's from other states came to visit.

LH's families were divided in their acceptance of Hathaway. His aunts and uncles were very accepting and reached out to make everything pleasant. On the other hand, certain members only tolerated her. She was never introduced to any of the city people, but, as was mentioned, their medical and Army buddies kept her and LH active.

Her high school classmate. Bertha, had married and lived in

the city. They revived their old school days friendship. One day on the streets, Hathaway met her girlfriend who lived next door when they were very young and Hathaway had torn up the friend's Easter outfit! They reminisced.

LH and Hathaway became very elated when Hathaway became pregnant. They were so excited! The excitement abruptly ended in three months with a spontaneous abortion. The next pregnancy ended the same way. The RH factor related to pregnancies was just becoming public. Hathaway had to acquaint herself with the new discovery that her blood type, A-RH Negative, was one in a thousand to become pregnant and usually with a complicated delivery. The babies' blood had to be replaced. Hathaway was shocked to learn that she was Type "A" because her dog tags in the Army had her blood type "O," good thing she did not need blood while in the service. As the old saying goes, "God takes care of babies and fools."

Hathaway's brother, Lenny came and stayed with her until he found work. He would clean the house and have meals prepared when she came from work. When he received his first pay check, he had to move out on his own. LH's brothers came home from the war. They moved in. His mother had to retire early because of illness. It was through her that LH and Hathaway had purchased their house from Martin Real Estate. The house, even with the use of the attic that had been remodeled into a recreation room to resemble the jungle area of New Guinea was becoming too crowded. Hathaway and LH were on a budget. She would purchase canned foods from the unclaimed freight houses where she had advised her patients to shop when she helped them to plan their budgets. At least there would be food from one pay day to the next even if she and LH only had perhaps a couple of dollars. No one contributed toward chores nor expenses for heat, lights and food. The bills became exorbitant. Their budget was blown to bits. Instead of being on top of things, it gave a feeling of being pushed down a barrel.

One weekend LH went to Illinois. He called Hathaway and asked her to chuck everything and come to Illinois. She just could not cop-out and leave her home. All of her Army money had been used to make the place comfortable. LH was an exceptional student and had no problems in accomplishing his goal, therefore she persuaded him to return home. But the home situations did not improve, nor were the problems on her job improving.

Cars, after the hostilities of war ended, were placed in a priority category for different professions. Since Hathaway was a nurse, she was given priority permission to purchase a car. The Chandler women gave her the down payment on the car. This was their first car, a Chevrolet, light blue. Hathaway arranged the Venetian blinds and looked at the new car for hours. The car came in handy that summer because her supervisor continued to assign Hathaway's cases far from her district.

Hathaway began to plan on how to cope with her problems. For the job problem, she would resign and seek employment with the City Public Health Department. The next morning in the office, the Supervisor assigned her a very severe case in one of the other districts. Hathaway told her she was not going to take the case. She told Hathaway that someone had to do it. Hathaway told her to take the damn bag and do it herself. Just then the head supervisor ran from her office and told Hathaway to shut up. Hathaway told her that she was an adult and to never tell her to "shut up." Hathaway used the phone to call the Director. She told the Director that she would like for her resignation to become effective one month from that date.

The Director told Hathaway to relax, drink a cup of coffee, then drive to her office. When Hathaway arrived, the Director told her that she did not approve of the segregation but the black doctors had asked that a couple of blacks become supervisors in a black office instead of demanding such steps be taken in an integrated setting; that she had been looking for a person with Hathaway's credentials and attitude to develop an integrated setting as assistant supervisor in all all-white down-river community. The next day Hathaway moved into the office in Dearborn until the new office was completed.

The experience in the new office was quite a challenge. The Assistant Supervisor from the black office would pass over Hathaway the papers that were distributed at supervisor's meetings, then she would remark, "Oh! I'm not accustomed to your attending the meetings." Some of the white clients in the new area would say how surprised they were to have a black nurse in their home and, by the same token, other were quite gracious and accepting. Student nurses aides were assigned to Hathaway for supervision of their practical application of Public Health Principles. There were wonderful opportunities to help families use improvised equipment and occasionally to develop special type equipment as needed. She was able to apply many of the principles she had learned the summer at the University of Minnesota. One of the black schools was in her district. This gave her contact with the young generation. She encouraged them to think well of themselves, and to develop their potentials in order to contribute to society and their community. Contact with some of the people, black and white, in these communities continues to this day.

With the change to a new setting, Hathaway was becoming very pleased but very depressed when it was time to go home. In-law problems were increasing instead of getting better. The brothers would collect the Army's twenty dollars a week bonus for fifty-two weeks and would not share one dime toward expenses. The family had begun to sabotage Hathaway's and LH's happiness and future plans.

Heavy snow was falling one Sunday morning. Hathaway had become fed up with the situations in her new house. She decided to leave. She packed her bags into the car and headed for Southern Illinois to the Chandler family's home. On the way a voice said to her. "Why be a fool? It is yours and LH's house. You are falling into a trap by doing exactly as they want you to do, and that is to leave." Hathaway thought again about her ridicule of the ministers who would say, "I heard a voice, etc.,". She turned the car around and went back to her house. LH was alone in the bedroom lying across the bed. His mother, sister and her family and brothers were in the kitchen eating Hathaway's Sunday dinner. Hathaway went into the bedroom and got her Army 45 revolver from a drawer and ordered them all, except the mother, out of her house immediately and called a locksmith to come and change the tumblers in the locks. All hell broke loose! LH's mother had told the sons that she had used their Army money to help buy the house. They believed her since she did not have the money that they had sent home. Hathaway told them the cancelled check and money order stubs where she and LH had purchased the house while they were stationed in the South Pacific were in Mr. Harris' safe deposit box.

Hathaway would never put LH's mother out. Where would she stay? What if this had been her mother in such a situation? How would she feel? Therefore, LH's mother continued living with them. The payment on the house was thirty-six dollars a month. Hathaway would give the payment to LH's mother to take to the real estate office since it would be closed by 5:00 p.m., when she left the job far away in the suburbs.

One day while riding in the district, Hathaway heard another voice or had a premonition, "Check your land contract when you get home." Upon arrival home, Hathaway immediately went to the desk drawer where she kept the bills. The land contract was not there. She asked LH where was it and he stated, "In the drawer." His mother ran from the bedroom and screamed, "I have it and I am going to see that you all are put out of my house like you put my boys out, because this is my house!" What Hathaway at the time didn't know was that she had kept the house payments at intervals and had told the real estate company to foreclose because she was going to return to work and that she would make the payments. The real estate company had sent a letter stating that the payments were in arrears. By her living in the house, she had destroyed the notice so that LH and Hathaway would not become wise to her scheme. She had ransacked the trunk in the attic looking for Hathaway's cancelled check of purchase and the money order stubs of LH's payment on this house. Fortunately Hathaway had placed these things in Mr. Harris' safety deposit box. (Harris is the man who grew up with her parents and had made Hathaway walk for the first time in her life for red pop. LH's mother had torn off the portion of the land contract that showed LH and Hathaway as owners and had taken the original copy to her lawyer to have LH and Hathaway evicted.

Hathaway had given her mother-in-law all of her mother's clothes, new articles from which tags were not removed. She had died before having a chance to wear some of the things. Whenever Hathaway bought anything for herself, she would buy something for her mother-in-law, so why was she doing all of these mean things to her? She did everything possible to break up the marriage. Hathaway began screaming and crying. She called the Chandler family in Illinois, who had helped her through the years, then she called Mr. Harris. He came immediately and proceeded to tell LH's mother that Hathaway was not alone in this city. He was there to protect her. Mr. Harris contacted his lawyer and paid the real estate company all of the arrear notes and six months advance payments. The lawyer paid five dollars to the real estate company to obtain a photostatic copy of the original contract for the house that showed LH and Hathaway as owners. The mother-in-law's lawyer was appalled. He had no idea they owned the house and that they were veterans.

Mr. Harris' lawyer wanted to press charges against Hathaway's mother-in-law. By this time Hathaway was confused, angry and ready to go to court. LH was confused so he took the easy way out, removed himself from the whole situation by re-enlisting into the service. He was discharged as a First Lieutenant and could have re-enlisted with the same rank but a time limit had expired. Therefore, he re-enlisted as a Sergeant. His career to become an accountant went down the drain. Since he had done exceptionally well in the course, the Department had made plans for him to begin the practical phase at the City Accounting Department. This procedure was an exception to the usual policy, but since LH was a junior and an A student, they bent the rule. Hathaway was very disappointed and angry with his family for creating such a turmoil within two years of their marriage.

Hathaway had experienced wary and uneasy feelings when things were going sour. What else could happen to them? LH's first assignment was not too far away. He and Hathaway could commute on weekends. Hathaway did not want to give up her home. All her life she had wanted a home of her own. This house was part of her now. It took a year of commuting and pleading from LH for her to chuck the house and join him at the Army base.

It took a catastrophe to help her to make up her mind to leave.

An Army buddy was visiting. In fact she had planned to move to the city to work in one of the local hospitals. When Hathaway awakened one morning, she was so angry with her mother-in-law for driving LH away that when the mother-in-law emerged from her bedroom, Hathaway grabbed her by the throat and began choking her until she turned blue...veins popped up...premonition again! Suppose someone did this to your mother; how would you feel? Hathaway's hands dropped;. Her buddy jumped out of bed, immediately began packing and caught the next train to Illinois and said, "Never would I be a witness to a murder!" LH and Hathaway had to send her trunk to Illinois when Hathaway decided to join LH at the Fort.

It seemed as if there would never be an end to the hatred. Her mother-in-law would make snide remarks, such as, "She never thought she'd give birth to a henpecked son," all because Hathaway handled all of the money and paid all bills; in fact, managed the household. No one would ever believe all the things that happened in this house; some were the same cruel actions and remarks that Hathaway had experienced when she was growing up in the small Southern Illinois town.

Finally Hathaway relented: The attic was converted into a studio apartment for LH's mother and the house was rented out to a girl who had known Hathaway when her great grandmother had placed her temporarily in an orphanage where this girl lived. Hathaway just knew that this girl would take good care of her house. She was never so misled. The house began to fall part. This girl never polished the beautiful hardwood floors nor kept the place clean. Rent was never paid on time. Finally, she was asked to move after owing six-hundred dollars in back rent. LH and Hathaway were absolutely disgusted and fed up with all of the troubles. Therefore, they sold the house to the neighbor next door. Years later Hathaway visited the house. The occupants had kept the house as she had; beautiful outside and inside. Wall-to-wall carpeting covered the beautiful hardwood floors, but that is today's trend. The bathroom tile still looked as new as the day it was installed.

Hathaway submitted her resignation to be effective in a month. One month, then LH and she would be together alone; no more hassles; requirements and finishing up last minute details before leaving filled Hathaway's day. It was the nights: lonely and empty without LH. She began to spend the nights reminiscing and having flashbacks!

During their nights together in the jungles of New Guinea...how they would hop the ditches filled with wild animals that separated the nurses and officers' quarters. One of the soldiers in the unit married and spent the honeymoon in their home. The matron of honor at her wedding came to visit and, since so many friends came, she had to share the bed with Hathaway and LH. During the night Hathaway and LH slept for awhile in the bathtub. The best man at their wedding and his wife would accompany Hathaway to the Fort every weekend so that she could cook. LH could not stand the mess hall food. She would cook everything on the barbeque stand. She even made blackberry dumplings occasionally for dessert. Then they would sneak away deeper into the woods or visit an Army buddy's home for a couple of hours. She lost a lovely umbrella in those woods.

One of the famous musicians, Jay Mac, from the Midwest knew Hathaway during her nurses' training days. He and his wife spent their honeymoon in LH and Hathaway's home. They had loads of fun reminiscing about those day and how at parties Hathaway would dance. The musician and his band played every weekend at the movie house's stage shows. They laughed about the night Hathaway caused all of Count Basie's men to be evicted at 3 a.m. because of her laughing at the wrong time. In the midst of these fun things, anger would take over when she flashed back over her mother-in-law's tribulations of voodoo books in sight; salt under the bed, snide remarks of "How do you think I feel when you finish eating and run in to the bedroom and leave me alone." Hathaway's answer was, "Find someone to run with into your bedroom," and then she would slam the door. Maybe some of this stress had contributed to her miscarriages. What if there had been children? Maybe LH would have thought twice about returning to the service.

Then there were the parties! One doctor who was stationed with them in the South Pacific, was practicing here. He would have lovely parties in his home. He would become drunk and then, either in his pjs, shorts, or smoking jacket, whichever attire struck him at the moment, would come downstairs and say, "Everyone out immediately except Hathaway and LH! They are my dear Army buddies. We were together in the jungles of New Guinea!" We would reminisce.

There was an episode of the ship taking the hospital units from new Guinea to the Philippines. One of the white nurses and an officer were necking on the deck. So were Hathaway and LH. The two couples were on their blankets when the wind became exceptionally high. The two nurses' heads became bumper to bumper as anchors! When they finally went below deck, everyone wanted to know where in the hell they had been. A warning of a typhoon had been issued and everyone was told to remain on one level. Boats, furniture, etc. were being washed overboard. Well, as the saying goes: "God takes care of babies and fools!"

Speaking of ships, Hathaway experienced the moving of a patient from a ship to her ship over the ocean by rope with the patient in a huge wicker-type basket. The air was tense among the staff for fear the atmosphere over the ocean and waves would cause the rope to snap. Everything came out okay in the end. The soldier needed emergency surgery.

The treacherous people in Southern Illinois! Elizabeth died before LH returned from the war. Hathaway took LH to her home to visit the Chandler family. They stayed in her mother's house that was without electricity and a bathroom. Hathaway cracked up when LH had to use the chamber pot! As usual some of the people could not resist telling him a bit of Hathaway's past...that she was supposed to have dated one of the local white doctors. LH told them that he had met Doctor Elkorn. They almost dropped their teeth! One lady stated that Hathaway's crying spells in the South Pacific was exactly what Elizabeth went through during that period also. She thought that one of her children was not going to return from the war. She had Hathaway and three sons in the service. All made it back okay.

Flashbacks included some of the pleasant activities in the Army and on the job as a Visiting Nurse in Michigan. One day she went on a maternity visit. A man answered Hathaway's knock on the door. He began laughing, falling out on the floor as he kicked and laughed. Hathaway thought to herself that she was supposed to give care to a newborn baby, not to a mental case. He said to his wife, "Get my album." She could not understand him in the beginning, consequently she too was becoming angry with him. Finally he got his album. There were two photos of Hathaway when she had practiced abandoning the ship and LH had to climb the rope to help her down. The wind had inflated her khaki pants over the buttocks and around the ankles where the pants legs were draped over high top shoes and white socks. They looked like the baggy pants of the Turks. This soldier had taken a front view to associate with the nurse's behind. He stated that he never thought that in a lifetime would he ever see Hathaway again. All had a big laugh. His wife was happy to have an opportunity to meet an Ex-Army nurse.

Also coincidentally, the doctor for this family and Hathaway had trained in the same hospital and Hathaway hated him. He was void of compassion, arrogant and conceited. Hathaway's first experience on the Maternity Unit was while he went to supper when a primipara went into labor. The doctor and nurse were to take Hathaway in on the case. The patient had not dilated; suddenly pain, groan and Hathaway checked the patient's amniotic fluid which sprayed into her face and hair. Hathaway's own urine went all over the place. She began screaming for help. A multiparous patient who knew everything going on in the ward, stuck her head in the door and stated she would have someone fetch the doctor. From a dry run orientation, Hathaway had presence of mind to follow the principals involved which she had learned in class. Consequently all went well. When this doctor arrived, he began laughing and said, "Now I guess you will hurry when the doctor is delivering." Under her breath Hathaway said, "Son of a bitch!" She had an opportunity to get even when the two were assigned to surgery. She damned near cracked his hand when she handed him instruments during surgery. The school paper wrote about the delivery and how she had to go off duty to shower and then go to the beauty shop. In later years when Hathaway became a visiting nurses in the city, this family was assigned to her district for child care visits. The mother would tease her and tell her son to come: the nurse who almost dropped him during his birth was here to check on his growth and developmental status.

She was far away from the city in the Midwest now, but some of the health problems were just the same on the present job. She had a female patient confined to a wheelchair. The husband had a home built with doors to accommodate a wheelchair for access throughout the house. The only problem was incontinence of urine. The woman loved to accompany her husband to many activities. Hathaway drew a pattern for panties to be made out of oil cloth. The patient's mother obtained the oil cloth and, with directions, made panties that solved the problem. There was no such thing as Depends and diapers on the market during the 40s. When Hathaway left the agency, on her last day, this patient prepared a delicious luncheon and even baked a cake. Recently, contact was resumed with this family.

In connection with another case, Hathaway had to smile when she made a home visit. The mother of the patient reluctantly admitted her into the home and stated she had never had a Negro in her home and she did not know what her small daughter might say to offend Hathaway. Hathaway told her that she did not become offended by statements from young ones; they were only stating what they learned from parents. The five-year old said, "We have never had a nigger in our house." Hathaway asked her if she would like to learn something...that the word, "nigger" was not a person but a bad act by a person. If she were to take her classmates' crayons, act mean to them, fight, steal, then she would be a nigger. Person who had brown skin are called NEGRO, repeat "Negro." People with different colors of skin were like the flowers surrounding her house; God made people different colors. She attended Sunday School every week. When Hathaway washed her hands, the child remarked that nothing came off of her hands. You are wearing lipstick like my mother's, etc. When her father drove up, the child almost broke the bay window knocking, yelling, "Daddy! We have a NEGRO in our house!" These flashbacks continued to help Hathaway through the lonely nights.

They were too poor to buy a cake and Hathaway had never

in her life baked a cake. They had a mincemeat pie with one candle in the center. Another episode occurred when she had lost the diamond wedding ring LH had his mother purchase and send to him in Manila. However, it did not arrived in time for the wedding. A year later she found the ring in the front yard after having been buried there in the grass for a year! When the sun hit it, the diamond began to sparkle.

One episode concerned their new car: Hathaway had driven the blue Chevy until it was about to fall apart. The Chevy Company had serviced the car for three years. The manager just knew it was in very good condition, and when Hathaway told him that she wished to have a new one, he said OK. Then he began to flirt by saying, "My wife is in Florida. Your husband is in the service. Why don't we go out to dinner one evening and have fun on the town?" Hathaway said, "Fine, but I want to trade in on a new car." Finally the papers were completed with no payment necessary with the trade-in. The mechanics knew the condition of the old car, and when they were ordered to get the black fleetline Chevy ready for her, they cracked up laughing because they knew the manager would have a fit when he finally checked the turn-in-car. Hathaway also knew this but the deal had been completed when she signed the papers. When the manager got downstairs and checked Hathaway's turn-in, he became furious. The seat was broken, Paint was going from the steering wheel. It was awesome. Hathaway asked him when would he pick her up for the dinner date. He said, "Like hell! You took advantage of me and I do not want ever to see you again!" Hathaway told him that he was the one who became carried away. She couldn't help it because he wanted to date her. Hathaway could hardly get away fast enough to call LH and tell him about the episode and that they had a new car. LH told his comrades that he had a new car and his wife would drive it up that weekend. They laughed at LH and said, "No way! Cars are still being rationed." LH told them that they didn't know his wife. They bet him $50.00 and almost fell out when they saw LH drive up in his new car!

Another incident that will long be remembered: One of the officers who was in the same medical unit in charge of troop work assignments, came to attend one of the auto company's classes in Michigan. He came to Hathaway's home and asked to stay a couple of days. LH had returned to the Army. Thank goodness he was not at home because this officer had done everything in his power to sabotage LH's assignments by not releasing the soldiers needed. A couple of days became two weeks. After that, Hathaway asked him to find a room for rent because he was tying up the guest room. Also, he would eat like a horse and not buy one morsel of food. Finally by two and half weeks, Hathaway got him out. He asked what would she like as a gift. She told him she did not wish anything. As he was going out the door, he turned and said, "Don't be surprised if I send you a jackass." She and LH have never seen the dumb SOB again.

What a loss to the accounting field, Eugene was sad when LH decided to leave college and return to the Army. Hathaway had to forget the money that an accounting position would have provided. But, a person must do what he thinks is best for himself. She had to agree with his instructors who said that he had a brilliant mind. Hathaway had enrolled in night classes at Wayne State. On a composition, she received a low grade and was irate because the instructor had evaluate it as "tripe." She was furious by the time she arrived at home. LH took over and rewrote the composition in a half hour. When she resubmitted the paper, the instructor gave it a grade of 90. She was fit to be tied. She had written the essay from her observations of autumn changes of color of tree leaves in the Bay City area of Michigan which reminded one of a fashion show. To Hathaway, the fashions were blended well with the colors of the leaves. The scenery was fantastic as she drove along the highways.

LH's classmates were disappointed when he re-enlisted, especially the men who had formed a club of classmen. They had one of their luncheons in his home and to show their appreciation, they gave him and Hathaway a set of tall stem, beautifully decorated crystal water glasses. LH and Hathaway still have those glasses.

Hathaway wondered what would have happened had she accepted the U.S. State Department offer to accompany the renowned black anthropologist who had taught tropical disease classes in New Guinea where she was stationed. Because of her Public Health background, he had requested her as a member on this staff to work toward eradication of malaria and other tropical diseases in Liberia. LH and she were quite elated when the telegram came to their home; to think she had been chosen. Of course she had to refuse now that she had married. She had to laugh over all of these offers she had received to live in other countries: first, Lt. Jackman's offer to live in Java, but as his wife; now Liberia on a research task team as a Public Health Nurse; Australia families wanted her to live there and practice nursing!

As time drew near for her to move, Hathaway became more apprehensive. She was not ready to give up her home which was what she had wanted all her life; her own place. Hathaway weighed the positive and negative aspects of beginning an Army life again. Had she not married, her plans were to become a career Army nurse. While she was in Australia, she had discussed this possibility with the Chief of the Army Nurses Corps. The chief's home was in a town ten miles from Hathaway's home in Southern Illinois. She invited Hathaway to lunch. Hathaway's immediate Chief Nurse at the time became very jealous and angry because she had not been invited. She made snide remarks to Hathaway that, since she knew all of the high brass people, she would bitch more than ever. Hathaway told her that she didn't need the support of high ranking people to help her because she knew she was a GREAT BITCH in her own right! She had challenged people and problems most of her life. Hathaway wondered why would she remember such an episode at a time like this.

Perhaps a return to Army life would fulfill her dream to see the world by traveling with LH as his dependent. Maybe removal from the present atmosphere of stress would quite her nerves. Then she and LH might have success with pregnancies, especially with the new medical procedure in correcting the problem caused by RH factors.

Who would replace her in her district? Would the person really take the time to understand her clients and continue to stress the importance of developing an attitude of confidence in themselves There were some clients who paid no more than 10 cents for a visit because they did not want something for nothing. Pride! By the same token Hathaway had to make some clients pay for their visits, especially when she saw number slips where they were spending dollars every day on the numbers. Yet they cried poor and broke when the insurance payments for a Public Health Nurse ran out. She was collecting at least one dollar a week, depending on their income, rather than give them free care. Several husbands worked at the auto plants and would squander the pay check on booze, numbers, gambling and, in one case, the husband would buy all different kinds of meats and food; all they could eat for a couple of days. Hathaway helped him with a budget. She met him on the job every pay day and would take him shopping for clothing, furniture, food and small gifts for each member in his family. After about a year of this, he had begun to understand and was ready to proceed on his own with minimum supervision. Now that she was leaving, would things continue to progress? She couldn't ask a nurse to go beyond her duties for such cases.

Hathaway told many of her patients how to purchase unclaimed freight canned foods. She taught that dented cans were safe but to check for punctured tops because the contents will be spoiled. Hathaway always bought the unclaimed which provided food from one pay day until the next. It if were up to her, most of the Blacks would stand on their own two feet and survive by the time she finished with them.

The last week on duty was a merry-go-round. Her patients had many surprises for her last days of duty. One wheelchair patient baked a cake and had cake and coffee ready when Hathaway arrived. Her co-workers had a delicious luncheon and gave beautiful farewell gifts. It was really a sad experience to leave such lovely people. They were like one big happy family.

Just before Hathaway left to join LH at the Army Base, her supervisor visited a dear friend who was the director of the Public Health Department in the city where this Army Base was located, Ft. Custer, Michigan. Mrs. M told the director that Hathaway was moving into town, that she was an excellent nurse and was her assistant supervisor, that in fact the department had used her to integrate a suburban area in Down River and the plan had worked beautifully. Apparently the director did not listen well when the word "integrate" was used because she told her friend Mrs. M. that a job would be waiting when Hathaway arrived. (When she arrived and the director saw this Negro in her office, immediately no job was available.)

Prior to the move, Hathaway moved her mother-in-law up in the attic recreation room which was converted into an apartment. She rented her home to one of the older girls who had lived in the orphanage in which Hathaway's grandmother had placed her when she had to take an emergency trip to St. Louis. She just knew that the older woman would take good care of her home. What a mistake!

In June 1948 Hathaway moved to the western city in Michigan to join LH at this Army Camp. She anticipated the move believing that a Public Health job was for her. What a rude awakening! When the director of Public Health Nursing met with Hathaway, she told her that the Association did not have enough money in the budget to hire her. Actually the director had not really listened to her friend's conversation when she explained that Hathaway helped to integrate and did not say that she was a Negro. "Blacks" now the terminology. At the time, it was "Negro."

Hathaway settled in the Army barracks apartment with twelve rooms. She began to look up old classmates and schoolmates from her Southern Illinois home. They had wonderful visits updating history of their lives since they were young children together. Her junior high school buddy had migrated there and had several children. They were elated to see each other after so many years had passed. Their past flashed before them and they laughed and laughed over the foolish things they had done.

Hathaway told the Army people and her friends about the episode over the Public Health job. No money in the budget indeed! Therefore she would apply for a position at the local Veterans Administration Hospital. Her home town people told her that they too at the VA would not hire a Negro nurse. They worked there and they had never seen a Negro nurse on the staff. Hathaway asked if there were any Negro nurses in the community who might apply. Further the VA would have to tell her why she would not be hired. After all she was a an Army nurse veteran of World War II.

The next day Hathaway went to the Personnel Office and asked for an application. She was immediately interrupted by the clerk who stated there were no vacancies in the laundry or kitchen at that time. Hathaway's anger flared. She told the clerk that if she had allowed her to finish her statement she would have known that she wanted a nurse's position application and not a damn application in the laundry or kitchen. Typewriters became silent. Eyes widened in surprise. A young man ran from the back section, grabbed Hathaway by the hand and said, "Please come in. We never had a nurse to come in and we need you.

Listen girl, get that application and bring it to me immediately." Then he called the chief nurse and said, "Guess what? We have a new nurse over here. When may we see her?" She could be heard from the phone saying, "Come as soon as possible because we need a nurse with Public Health credentials to supervise a federally funded research project and Hathaway could coordinate the research on the tuberculosis unit." The Streptomycin Committee Research Office was in Washington, D.C. This was a project to evaluate the effectiveness of medication and para-aminosalicylic acid and streptomycin in eradication of tuberculosis.

All kinds of problems developed with the staff. The secretary had never worked for a Negro. A couple of the attendants were not going to work under the supervision of a Negro. They were all told to leave or work under the new nurse's supervisor. Ultimatums ended with the ward clerk typing anything Hathaway handed even if it were a scrap of paper. The attendants bent over backwards to accommodate and carry out all orders immediately in order to keep their jobs because they were told they were replaceable whereas a nurse was not, especially a very highly qualified nurse.

The young doctor assigned to the research project also went through hell with jealousy on the part of the older doctors who resented his having been chosen to head this project. Hathaway had to act as a buffer between the doctors. The young doctor had an arrested case of TB. Years later when it reactivated, Hathaway referred him to one of her former TB instructors at Minnesota. He helped the young doctor through his crisis and on to a new job assignment.

In this hospital were many qualified black men working as attendants to supplement their college tuitions. Some of those very men are now in the business and political areas in Michigan. One black social workers is now head of a department in a university in Michigan. One of the recreational Black men was married to the secretary for the chief nurse.

The patients became very active in the project. Hathaway began to plan many recreational activities. Birthdays were celebrated with live music on the patios, whereas before people were afraid of tuberculosis and would not come near the unit. Once Hathaway finished teaching isolation techniques for methods of protection, everything began to fall in place. Soft music was played everyday during rest periods. She wore out three records of Clair de Lune. One day, one of the psychiatric patients in the research project came to her office door and said, "Bitch, are you playing that record for us or for yourself?" Hathaway had to laugh.

Hathaway's hometown schoolmates and friends could not accept her good fortune in breaking the segregated ways at the hospital because they never called nor visited once she was hired. One of her dear friends when they were growing up was pregnant when Hathaway visited her. When Hathaway returned several months later and saw the baby, she was surprised and asked her friend whose baby it was. Her friend told her that it was hers and since she, Hathaway, was so goddamn smart, a nurse and an educated woman, she should have know that she was pregnant when she came to visit upon her arrival in town. Hathaway cursed her out, left and has never seen this supposed friend since.

Hathaway survived the attitudes and treatment from her Southern Illinois townspeople, went on about her business, met new friends and lived happily during LH's assignment at the Army Base Friends from Detroit and Army wives' activities kept time moving.

The Secretary for the chief nurse and Hathaway became very close friends. One day when the secretary returned home from work, she was confronted by the landlady who wanted her to vacate the apartment immediately. Where could she find a place to move with such a short notice? Hathaway and LH lived in a fourteen room Army barracks and they went to her rescue. The secretary, her husband, young baby and mother-in-law moved in with LH and Hathaway.

One evening when Hathaway returned home, the baby was crying. When Hathaway checked his diaper, she found dark red blood. She had the mother call the doctor and informed him to meet her, baby and Hathaway at the hospital. The baby was diagnosed as having Sickle Cell Anemia. Hathaway recalled her experience with the patient during her nurses training days in the 30's. During WW II, the condition became nationally know because Black soldiers with Sickle Cells began to black out when flying at high altitudes.

Within two years, the research project was finished. One of Hathaway's nurse schoolmates came and she was immediately given a charge nurse position over the Acute Unit of the hospital.

Two years later LH was assigned to Korea. Hathaway made plans to re-enter the University of Minnesota School of Public Health on the GI Bill for veterans. She had attended the summer before entering the Army Nurse Corps in 1942. Now she was ready to obtain the degree.

She had attended night classes at Wayne State when she lived in Detroit and continued in the University of Michigan continuation night classes when she moved to the VA Hospital area. The experience at the University of Minnesota was most rewarding and gratifying for Hathaway. Most of the instructors were also veterans. They were interested in their students. When Hathaway found some classes rather difficult, the instructors counseled her and in one class even obtained a tutor. She was the first full-time Negro student to be admitted to the School of Public Health in the undergraduate program. She was a very ambitious student and never let obstacles stand in her way. A very determined person, Hathaway evaluated the assistance given and recognized the falsity of statement that in a larger institution as student is merely a number and especially when Negro students are concerned.

The Army Nurse Corps recalled Hathaway since she was in in the reserve to enter the Korean crisis. Orders were issued and plans for furniture and car storage had been made. The University of Minnesota's Dean of the School of Medicine Public Health Department sent a letter to Washington that a degree would prepare Hathaway to be more efficient in her field and valuable to the Army Nurse Corps as a graduate. The orders were rescinded and Hathaway was given permission to continue at the university.

During spring break, Hathaway accompanied the political science group to New York for sessions at the United Nations which was at the time housed at Lake Success in New York. Students from all the eastern colleges were in attendance. These students were from all over the world. Hathaway had a reunion with Lt. Templeton. She had not seen him since they were separated at Fort Huachuca where they had planned to marry. It was the happiest reunion two people could ever experience. Time was too short.

In a couple of days the students had to leave for Washington, D.C. for a tour and sessions at the White House. Congressman Hubert Humphery had breakfast for all of the University of Minnesota students. Next day, Hathaway left to visit friends in Portsmouth, Virginia, then back to join the group in Washington for the trip back to Minnesota.

Hathaway had been considered a pledge for one of the most outstanding sororities and became a member in 1951. That year the sorority planned to have a formal dinner dance. Hathaway was excited because Lt. Templeton had promised to escort her to the affair. Later the sorors decided the pledges would be maids and waitresses at the affair. No way would Hathaway have Templeton come to the affair and not have her as his date. He had sent a telegram that he had to attend an uncle's funeral in Dallas and would come immediately to Minnesota. Hathaway called his apartment in order to catch him before he left for Dallas. He had gone and his girlfriend would not give any information. Hathaway had the operator give phone numbers of all the Negro mortuaries in Dallas. She reached Templeton and told him not to come to Minnesota for the affair and also how the girlfriend had been profane and rude. The girlfriend never understood why her affair immediately broke up in their relationship. She had no idea how much Hathaway's friendship meant to Templeton.

Hathaway decided to move onto the campus. Ironically, Hathaway's roommates were white. All three were Aries. One roommate was a veteran Army nurse, had been stationed in the same South Pacific area, participated in the same Christmas festivities in Australia as Hathaway, but since the Army was segregated, they never met. Now, they were roommates and majoring in the same Public Health program. The other roommate was a young student from Indiana. Her father was a doctor and came to the campus to take all three Aries girls out for a birthday dinner. When they arrived at the swanky restaurant, the Maitre'D stated that he was sorry but he had no vacancies. The doctor identified himself and stated he had reservations and wanted them immediately over by the large bay windows overlooking the sidewalk. They were promptly seated and the four of them had a big laugh. Hathaway and the two roommate continued through the years to visit and keep in touch.

The Public Health degree required Hathaway to do a course of practice teaching on the agriculture campus. Her bacteriology instructor assisted her in developing her lesson plans. For rural type of living the required trips of observation with a sanitarian and an engineer were most helpful in writing her lesson plans, especially when it came time to discuss the use of Imhof type toilets, their place of location and the building of expansion type of house for future family development.

Her supervisor thought the class sessions were excellent. The next summer Hathaway had to go to the Topeka, Kansas, Health Department for practical applications of public health principles. It was in this city that Hathaway met many of the sorors, had observations at Meninger's Clinic and an opportunity to visit with ex-Army comrades that she had served with in the South Pacific during World War II.

Graduation was near. Hathaway's classmates obtained her cap and gown and had everything ready for her return from Topeka.

LH returned from Korea just in time for Hathaway's graduation. Her ex-Public Health field teacher during nurses' training attended the graduation. She had been instrumental in Hathaway's being hired by the Visiting Nurses Association in Missouri. She was quite proud of Hathaway's endeavors and became kind of a second mother to her. (In later years when she became ill, Hathaway went to her aid. In 1979 she died of cancer; quite a loss to Hathaway.) LH had an opportunity to meet most of Hathaway's instructors. Relationships with several of the instructors continued through the years.

LH received an assignment in Maryland. Hathaway returned to the VA Hospital in Michigan to wait until LH found living quarters in Maryland. Approximately three months later. Hathaway made plans to move to Maryland with an assignment as Senior Public Health Nurse for the state. She was elated over joining LH and having secured a job.

All hell broke loose when she arrived in Maryland. The doctor who examined Maryland State employees was recently hired; the first one had died. When Hathaway went to him for the examination, she entered the waiting room, sat and looked through the magazines. The doctor saw her in his reserved FOR WHITE ONLY WAITING ROOM and ordered her to go and sit on his back steps; that Negroes waited in the back on the steps. Hathaway told him she would not sit on his damn back steps; he could go to hell. He informed her she could not work for the state without his examination. She told him that she didn't have to work for the state and left his office. The Health Department was shocked, now aware of the doctor's attitude and procedure. The director asked Hathaway if she'd reconsider the job if they were to get another physician to do the examination. She was to consider this over the weekend.

Hathaway returned home to LH, angry over the episode of the day but quite elated over being united with LH. He had written prior to her move to Maryland that he had become involved with a lady but maybe he and Hathaway could clear up their problem. If not, then maybe they should divorce.

The elation was short-lived as the saying goes. "Absence makes the heart grow fonder for somebody else." LH had met a lady in a bar one night and both needed someone to fill their feeling of loneliness. The lady and her husband had divorced. Hathaway was apparently interested in a career and marriage would hinder her progress so LH thought. So he and the lady became involved in a love affair. She became so excited and in love with LH that she was going back to school to take a secretarial course so that she could help him when they got married.

LH took the weekend off to make a trip with his lady friend because it had been planned before Hathaway arrived and he was not about to stand her up. Hathaway was irate. Two episodes within a week was just too much - the doctor about the physical examination and LH keeping his date with the new lady.

These two episodes blew Hathaway's mind. She called the Chandler family in Southern Illinois. Her mentor flew out to Maryland. Hathaway's ex-boyfriend, Lt. Templeton took the train from New York into Maryland. He told Hathaway that she must have loved LH because she broke their engagement to marry him. He felt the same way LH felt, that marriage would hinder her from an ambitious career although he still loved her and would always be around if she needed him. Between the two, they were able to help Hathaway through the crisis. She had never been the victim of such actions for she was the one who always walked away from a situation. Her ego was hurt.

That Monday Hathaway had the physical examination by the new state physician. She took the job as senior Public Health Nurse and moved in with a private family. Within two weeks, LH had orders for Europe and asked Hathaway to join him there. One day he called from Europe to ask her to come to him; to please forgive him and his actions; that he really loved her so please come to Europe. He didn't know that she had plans to take advantage of that opportunity to go to Europe. She would never be the victim of a situation again in life. She had always wanted to visit Europe and decided this would be one way of doing so. The Army would send for her. How could she lose? She became excited over the fact that, at last, she would have an opportunity to see Paris. All through high school she wanted to be a French teacher and visit Paris and one day she was going there. She recalled that her French teacher in the tenth grade failed her in French all because she wanted Hathaway to live up to their predictions that she wasn't going to be anything in life but would have a house full of bastards like her mother. Thank God, Miss Chandler rescued Hathaway by taking her to the school she taught in and helped her to make it in life. Her dreams were continuing to materialize.

Looking on the bright side of life, Hathaway settled in on her job. Her district assignment included four schools in the area. Each district of the Public Health Department had to conduct in-service programs on a rotating schedule. Hathaway's district was scheduled, she was elected chairman of the program.

Hathaway developed a play, wrote the script, designed the costumes and filmed the play. The play was called "The Forgotten Child." The play depicted the Public Health Nurse's visit to a pregnant mother and, during the visit, she observed the actions of the preschooler, a very lonely child. The Health Department office was integrated but home visits remained segregated. Negro nurses only visited Negro homes and white nurses only visited white homes.

"The Forgotten Child" film was integrated. Hathaway had a Negro nurse visit a white pregnant mother. The lonely child was repeating the poem, "A Preschooler's Thought," which was published in the "New Yorker" magazine in the late forties. The film was such a success that the Maryland Mental Health Association wanted to use it at the opening session of their state conference.

One day Hathaway's supervisor called the office and revealed her plans to accompany Hathaway on her visits into the homes the following day. It was time for Hathaway to receive a rating on her job performance. The supervisor was a Canadian. The first home visit was to a tuberculosis patient. He was an avid reader and had one room set up like a library with many books. When Hathaway began to discuss his progress, he interrupted by asking a questions: "Why do the doctors have conflicting diagnoses about my case? One day I do not have TB, yet your doctors say I do. They are just like the conflicting versions found in the Bible. Young lady, can you explain these problems? You do read the Bible, don't you?" Hathaway said to herself, "Oh, Uh." The University of Minnesota that had required the Public Health students to take literature of the Bible because of the cross-section of populations they would encounter religious questions. Hathaway began explaining that people of today are like those people in the biblical days who transcribed or translated the cross. Each person reads and translates as to what it means to him. No two people interpret a message the same. True, in those days, people had eye diseases the same as today, candle light or torches only, no electricity as of now. The Greek invasion brought vowels into the language and one little mark on an already established method would change the complete translation of the word. With this kind of knowledge, the patient stated he was beginning to understand a little better and he would follow through in coming to the clinic. When they left his home, the supervisor jumped all over Hathaway; that the policy is not to discuss religion with the patient and he no doubt did not understand a word she had spoken. Hathaway jumped back and asked her how long had it been since she had been back to college for a refresher course. The POLICY is not to coerce a person to change his religion from Catholicism to Protestantism or vice versa but one can discuss intelligently the principles of religion; that the patient was no dummy. He no doubt had a wider range of reading than she or Hathaway.

The next visit was to a home where Hathaway had listened to all kinds of blues records to establish a rapport with the mother in order to get her to bring the daughter in for fitting of new braces. The mother had not returned to the clinic because she felt they were not nice to her because she was a Negro. Hathaway had built up her confidence and progress was in order. Upon entry into the house, the little girl began to cry. The supervisor asked, "What's wrong; are you afraid of the white face?" Her mother bristled. Hathaway had to calm her down with all kinds of gestures and eye contact and got the supervisor out immediately. Once outside, Hathaway told her off. The people are not heathens and she had just torn down six months of effort to get that mother to agree to return to the orthopedic clinic. Then the supervisor wanted to know why white children had head lice and Negro children had ringworm of the scalp.

Later when the supervisor wrote Hathaway's efficiency report, she stated that Hathaway needed to apply more regulations and policies of the department. Hathaway let her have it and refused to sign until she wrote clarification and justification of her statements which she could not and she ended by writing a fair evaluation. She was told that two visits were insufficient to evaluate nine months of work. She as asked what about the film Hathaway had written and produced for the Mental Health Hygiene Clinic.

Although the job was interesting, Hathaway was anxiously awaiting the time when she could leave for Europe. She met many friends, began to take weekend trips to Atlantic City beaches, stroll on the Boardwalk area and visit night clubs. In the sand on the beach is where she lost her gold watch gift from the VA staff when she left for Maryland. In one of the night clubs, she met one of the world's great guitarists whom she had known in her teens when he was a regular at Bellman and Writer's Club in St. Louis, Missouri.

Many beautiful weekends were spent in New York with Lt. Templeton. He entertained her and her co-workers whenever they visited the city. She became active in her sorority and when she left for Europe, they gave her a lovely jewel box with the sorority's colors. She has that gift today.

The doctor, during Hathaway's Nurses' Training was her instructor in Anatomy and Physiology, was now practicing and living here in Maryland. He introduced her to his family. Many happy weekends were spent with his wife and children.

Living in Maryland gave Hathaway an opportunity to frequently drive to New York to attend operas, plays and jazz sessions. When she walked into one of the night clubs, Ben Webster, world renowned Saxophone player, stopped in the middle of his program, ran down and greeted Hathaway with hugs and kisses. Ben was a cousin to Hathaway's classmate in Nurses' Training. In Philadelphia, she went to the musical that presented the Nicholas Brothers. Hathaway had danced with Fayett Nicholas at Ft. Huachuca. He was happy to see her. Ella Fitzgerald, Nat King Cole, and Pearl Baily with her husband, Belson were on the program. They all had a lovely after glo session. Hathaway's musical gang included Johnny Hodges, Count Bassie, Duke Ellington, Billie Holiday, Fay Terrell, Jimmy Rushing, Ray Nance, Paul Gonzales (his son is now a musician). Most of the gang have now left this world. On a visit to LH in Virginia at the Army Camp, Hathaway had to nurse Billie Holiday. Hathaway and LH were friends of Oscie Davis and Ruby Dee. His brother taught at the University in Florida with LH and Hathaway. Friendships that began during WW II at Ft. Huachuca with Lena Horne, continued for years.

When Hathaway and husband first settled in Detroit, she visited many of the clubs in Black Bottom and danced with Ziggy

Johnson.

Hathaway immediately began taking private German lessons since she was not planning to wait for the Army to send her to Germany because it would take too long.

All told, she had worked nine months and when her schools closed for the summer, she would resign the job and take the SS America ship to Europe. Nine months of German had equipped her with enough to drive across Germany since she had planned to take the car on the ship with her.

Three other Negro women were on board. They all registered to eat at different settings, however, the chief steward gave them the last setting together by the swinging doors from the kitchen. These women had never met before boarding the ship. Hathaway had a first class ticket but was placed in second class with one of the Negro women. They became very disgusted and irate with the chief steward. Hathaway refused to accept his arrangements and went in to discuss the issue. He pretended he was intoxicated, stated the steamship lines president had written that we all wished to be together. Hathaway told him that he and the president were liars because the women had never seen each other before this trip. The assistant chief came in and the chief steward began speaking in German, that this woman did not wish to sit with the other black women in the dining room. When Hathaway responded in German, asking him why was he discussing the issue with the assistant, the chief steward sobered immediately and asked where had she learned German. She did not give him the benefit of knowing that she had had a tutor but instead told him that German was taught in the American schools.

Before the ship docked, a Yeoman had typed for Hathaway a letter to the steamship lines president. LH met Hathaway in Bremerhaven. He would have to have Army papers to pick up the car. Therefore, he and Hathaway had to take the train across Germany to his base near Frankfurt and the next day when he reported into his office, there were the papers to pick up the car. That meant a long train ride back to Bremerhaven.

A German friend had told LH about an apartment for rent with a German family. Since Hathaway had left the states before the Army sent for her to join LH in Germany, they would have to live on the German economy. Six months later they moved into Army quarters.

Living with the German family was fantastic. The German lady would not allow Hathaway to speak English. Her husband would get anything Hathaway needed, even American cigarettes. Omar, the grandmother, lived in the home. She made delicious pastries. They all had a beautiful relationship by exchanging recipes, cultural foods, ideas, activities, special holidays and birthdays. They gave Hathaway many gifts of crystal and silver. This was the silver center of the world. Tiffany people from New York came here for training in silver craft. The steamship company removed the steward off the ship, sent Hathaway a letter of apology and refunded her ticket money. Hathaway took the money to buy her china. Her German family knew the Rosenthal family and got china for Hathaway at wholesale price. (The dishes had a gold and platinum band). They gave Hathaway sterling salad forks and spoons to match her place settings given as a wedding present from her Australian mother in Brisbane. Ironically, the German husband and wife were Aries with Hathaway so the month of March was spent with one birthday party after another and the exchange of lovely gifts.

The young son would bring his dog each morning into Hathaway's apartment and have her to shake his paw as he said, "Guten Morgan." Finally he taught Hathaway to like dogs. She had not liked pets when she was growing up, especially cats, and to this day, she has a horror of cats.

This relationship has lasted through the years. They continue to write in German, telephone and visit regularly. Hathaway continued German lessons from a private German teacher. She and Hathaway attended German operas and a German-American club that operated to promote relationships between the countries.

Hathaway applied for a Public Health Nurse's position with the American Civil Service Civilian Section. The Army needed a clinic in the suburb for Army civilians and dependents. This clinic was to alleviate the overflow in the Frankfurt clinic. The personnel officer called long distance to Hathaway and offered her the position, gave the date for processing and an appointment with the Colonel for finalization of her duties.

Hathaway went into Frankfurt to the central office. The German clerk fingerprinted her and finished typing the necessary salary papers. Hathaway then went to the Colonel for the last review. She waited and waited. Finally the Colonel came out to the secretary's desk and asked if Ms. Hathaway had arrived. The secretary looked surprise and said, "Sir, there is Ms. Hathaway and she had been waiting since 1:00 P.M., her scheduled appointment with you." The Colonel, an ex-polio patient walked with a limp. When he saw that Hathaway was Black, he almost fell; his face became very red, ("Will I have to resuscitate him?") He composed himself and said, "Come in, have a seat. You are not a graduate from Minnesota's School of Public Health. They do not allow Negroes into that program." Hathaway said, "Sir, now they do and I am the first nurse to graduate. You have my credentials before you." The Colonel said, "Well, we have more applicants to interview, so you'll be hearing from us; good day." Hathaway told him that she thought she would have to resuscitate him when he became so red and grey. He turned grey all over again! She laughed and said, "Good-by, Sir." (Resuscitation at that time was mouth to mouth.)

Hathaway was angry as hell when she drove home. She told LH that the conference was a disaster and that the colonel was a prejudiced bastard, etc.

Hathaway was to check with the personnel office each week. Each time she called he gave a flimsy excuse. She missed out on a tour to Spain just because he kept putting her off with lies. Finally he told Hathaway that they had no idea that she was a Negro when they read her application as a graduate from the University of Minnesota; sorry, but they gave the job to a white nurse who was an Air Force Public Health Nurse, to come in and set up the clinic. Hathaway was damned angry and immediately wrote a letter to the Civil Service Commission Federal Department in Washington, D.C.

A couple of weeks later, the Air Force Public Health Nurse arrived. She attended the sessions to get the clinic off the ground. In these sessions, the colonel referred to Hathaway as a nigger graduate from the University of Minnesota School of Public Health. He did not know that the nurse knew Hathaway. After the sessions she immediately drove to Hathaway's home and brought all of her notes because she knew Hathaway was going to write to Washington.

Two weeks after her return to the United States, the Civil Service Commission in Washington D.C. sent a letter about the investigation into Hathaway's refused employment after they found out she was a Negro and apologized for having put her through the situation, but the Civil Service Officers are given the last word.

In the meantime, the American Red Cross director had in earlier years attended the same integrated school Hathaway attended when she was living with her grandmother in a Northern Illinois town (Danville). He contacted Hathaway and asked if she would set up the clinic under the auspices of the Red Cross before the Army could begin. Hathaway wanted to retaliate, therefore she accepted. On a volunteer basis she began to organize. Since her Red Cross certificate had expired, she enrolled two days late in the already in-session Red Cross class. When Hathaway entered the Red Cross Class, the instructor greeted her in his very thick Southern drawl. She said to herself, not again, another prejudiced cracker! She didn't even give him a chance. He was very receptive and polite. There was one other Negro dependent in the class. Her husband was an officer and LH was a noncommissioned officer. The whole week of class she acted indignant toward Hathaway. Hathaway smirked to herself and said, "The stuck-up wench doesn't know that I am a nurse and chairman of the Red Cross outpatient clinic about to be developed in the area.

The day the classes ended, the instructor had all of the Army dignitaries and their wives present for the graduation. He called each student one-by-one for her certificate. He skipped over Hathaway. She began to think and to herself said, "I was right, he is a prejudiced person after all." Then came the last name on his list. He very loudly and clearly said, "Ms. Hathaway, the most outstanding student of the class." Immediately the doors flew open, photographers rushed in to take pictures as the deputy commissioner presented to Hathaway her certificate and announced her position on the Red Cross Volunteer Program. Later the instructor went over to Hathaway and said, "I know evil thoughts were going through your mind when I made you last on the list. I wanted a picture of your expression." They had a big laugh. The other Negro woman came over and said, "After all your should have been the best because you are a nurse and I am not." Hathaway told her that her white buddies in the class were also nurses and asked didn't she know that, and rudely walked away from the lady.

Hathaway began to meet with medical, Army staff and Red Cross staff to develop plans for the clinic. She organized immunization clinics, prenatal clinics and school health services for Army dependents. The wives responded well for the school health services. Those who were nurses assisted the doctors. Mothers and non-nurses monitored the lines of children and assisted the teachers. The school health services was the first such program for Army dependents' schools in Europe. The National Red Cross asked Hathaway to visit other Army bases and help them develop such programs in their area. They wanted to fly her as far as Africa to help the Red Cross develop the same type of program.

Hathaway taught the first aid and prenatal classes. Some first aid classes were taught at odd hours especially for Army ski instructors. Later - One of the ski persons, after his Army assignment, became a ski instructor in Colorado. The program was highly publicized throughout European army bases through the Stars and Tripes. Hathaway was sent to Red Cross conferences. The staff from Frankfurt was in attendance also. She would wait until coffee breaks, then invade the line, look at the Frankfurt representatives, smile sweetly and said "Hello." They would become so embarrassed! This made Hathaway feel very elated over the opportunity to embarrass the hell out of them in public. The staff from Frankfort included the colonel who had denied Hathaway the job when he found out that she was black.

One of the young pregnant girls in Hathaway's class came from Pennsylvania. Her husband was a young lieutenant. Her father was a doctor and he and his wife came over to visit their daughter. The daughter introduced them to Hathaway and told her father how much she had benefited from the classes. When she delivered, her father called Hathaway and asked if she'd teach his daughter privately how to take care of his grandson because he and his wife were returning to the United States and he would pay her price. Hathaway took the responsibility after her Red Cross volunteer hours.

Later when the baby was older, the parent moved him, maid and all into Hathaway and LH's home while they went on a month skiing trip. When Hathaway took the baby and maid to the commissary to shop, people would ask where she had gotten the baby. One of her white Noncommissioned Wives Club members asked her if she had lost her mind to adopt a white baby. Hathaway had to laugh but would not give her the satisfaction of explaining the deal involved.

Hathaway was president of the Non-Commissioned Wives Club and was sent as delegate to the conventions. She was active in the German-American Club and chairman of their welfare section. The activities of this section were, during the summer, to bring the East Zone children to the West Zone for the summer, place them in American and German homes and plan summer activities, then return them to their homes for school.

Hathaway was sent as delegate to the German-American Club Convention. It was German custon for the lines of representatives to welcome the delegates. The men would click their heels and kiss the back of the hand of the female delegates. All except one old German, who, when he got to Hathaway, clicked his heels and blew on Hathaway's hand. Later, she said, "she should have hit him in his mouth and stated that the air excited her."

Hathaway continued to represent the American Red Cross and NCO Wives Club at conventions. It was at one of these conventions that she had an opportunity to develop a friendship with the now deceased James Connant, ambassador to Germany. She and others, with Ambassador Connant, made tours of the German schools' classrooms and discussed the system.

The Red Cross throughout Europe and Africa requested Hathaway's services in helping them to develop health services in their areas. Hathaway did not have the time to follow through on such a wide range program. Also, she was the OB-GYN instructor for her health program and first-aid classes. Along with these volunteer duties, she was sandwiching in tours of public health departments in other countries in order to collect data for a Master's Degree Thesis.

Hathaway and LH decided to take a short vacation into the countries surrounding Germany. The first stop of the trip was Hamburg, Germany. The most exciting things in Hamburg were the night clubs with the nude showgirls jumping into flaming water. Hamburg was a beautiful city where one could find anything in the world.

In Amsterdam, Netherlands, prostitutes were beautiful women in most colorful designers' flowing gowns poised in the big bay windows along the canal that runs through the entire city.

Hathaway and LH stayed at a beautiful hotel located directly on the canal. The veranda afforded an excellent overview of the city. Tours of the smallest house in the world and the apartment occupied during the war by Ann Frank and families were most unique. Beautiful banks and banks of tulips glowing in the sunlight as they reflected on the library wall made the most beautiful picture in the world.

By boat they took a tour of Volendam where the factory of Deft Blue China is made. The place was overflowing with tourists buying everything in sight-tiny to large wooden shoes. The tour continued by boat to Marken Island that was settled several years before WW II by sixty families from other countries and had now expanded to a population of six-hundred. Men had left for the war. Some had returned. Others had married outside women and were forbidden to return to the island. To marry outside of the clan was a NO NO. Hathaway inquired about the public health aspects. By being surrounded by water, the island had a high percentage of TB. Incestous marriage? Eye conditions were not the only problems that was related to incest. So the doctor stated: The population resented the Netherlands Health Ministry supervisor. Consequently a health team headed by a doctor was only allowed to stay six months at the most on the island. The people wore Dutch custom type clothing, wooden shoes, men in bloom type knickers, women were not dressed too differently from Western fashions. The clothes were washed and rolled very tightly, then stored on side board type dressers.

All of the dishes were hung on the walls. Beds were bunks inside of a wall with curtains hanging over the entrance, same as curtains over windows.

Hathaway went back to Amsterdam for a couple more flings at nightlife, then off to Paris with stops along the way, one overnight in Anaheim where a circus had been shown internationally on TV. The journey continued on into an overnight in Verdum with a tour of the historical sights and cemetery of WWI soldiers. Next stop was in Paris where she obtained a room in one of the hotels off the bank of the Seine area across from the University of Paris Medical School. Hathaway and LH took in sights at the Louvre, Notre Dame, Arch de Triumph, Eiffel Tower, Lido Night Club with strobe lighting, Palace of Versailles, Pig Alley and many famous night clubs. Paris had the only health department and clinic that refused Hathaway an interview with the director. Hathaway waited at one of the sidewalk cafes until the director went to lunch, then doubled back to talk to the nurses. Things were dishevelled, cluttered and dirty. The director returned in the midst of the conversation and was very angry. He told Hathaway that if she wished to know about the health problems and so forth to go to the American Hospital. (It is called American Hospital in Paris.) Hathaway was very disappointed about Paris, the environment, cluttered, buildings, dirt, and people were discourteous, refusing to speak English. To think, during Hathaway's high school years she wanted to be a French teacher and live in Paris. She never remembered any geography except that of Paris. Someday as a French speaking person she would move to Paris-her dream world. After all of the past years, she had hated her French teacher for flunking her the first six weeks, but then another teacher, who was aware of Hathaway's abilities, had taken her out of the school and Hathaway commuted with the teacher to another city. Latin was the foreign language in this school so Hathaway had to switch to Latin. She never forgave the French teacher. Now she was in her dream world and what a let down...two disappointments. First her high school French teacher; now this horrible experience actually in Paris. As the saying goes: "God works in mysterious ways." Lack of money for a four year college degree with a major in

French had caused Hathaway to re-evaluate her desires and choose another profession. The chosen profession eventually made the way possible for a happy army nurse experience and a satisfactory marriage which offered her the opportunity to travel all over the world. Now she could see and speak to her former French teacher without bitterness. Hathaway had no more desire to return to Paris. In recent years, the buildings have been sand blasted and cleaned. The people are more courteous and speak English. Hathaway satisfied her desire to speak a foreign language by studying German at the Overseas University of Maryland in Germany. She has since visited Europe numerous times but never bothered to return to Paris.

By the last night in Paris, Hathaway had walked all day and was very tired. LH decided he would do one more night about town. Hathaway was happy for him to go out alone because she was the keeper of their money (so she thought). As she peeked out the window to watch LH walk down the street, he suddenly stopped, bent over and took money from his sock! He sure pulled a fast one or so he thought. Hathaway found the trick amusing.

They drove and went by a boat-train to Copenhagen. The trip was most delightful. Upon arrival, Hathaway and LH obtained a room through the registers at one of the tourist offices for a Danish home. The Danish couple and their little boy lived in an apartment complex opposite the first-of-its-kind worldwide senior citizen apartment buildings.

From the reception and greeting extended, one would have thought Hathaway and LH were long lost relatives returning home. Language was no barrier, communication went beautifully inspite of the fact that the family spoke only Danish.

Hathaway and LH spoke only English. The couple's little blonde, blue-eyed five year old stood in awe at the beginning but in less than an hour he was climbing all over LH,and he took LH on a tour of the neighborhood. He was fascinated with LH's Oldsmobile 88 and posed for pictures at all angles, The tragedy of this acquaintance was that a couple of years later, Hathaway lost their address. Consequently, communication through correspondence ended.

Hathaway and LH were touring a section of Copenhagen and

stumbled upon a place called "Wonder Bar." LH suggested they check it out. A group had come for a reunion and were celebrating when they saw Hathaway and LH enter. They immediately included them in the celebration. In the meantime, the discussion of Hathaway's possession of a letter of introduction to Copenhagen's Public Health Department took priority. They called the department, made the appointment and were given explicit directions to the office.

The next day, Hathaway and LH were guests of the Ministry of Health with luncheon and a tour. Hathaway received valuable information from the director and nurses in the Public Health Department. This information would be most valuable as a comparative study if and when Hathaway decided to pursue a Masters Degree in Public Health Nursing.

Having been exposed to the culture of Scandinavia at the University of Minnesota, Hathaway knew what to expect. Food galore! One would have thought that she had never eaten a morsel of food in her life the way she ate at the smorgasbord restaurants and Danish pastry bakeries.

She went to Sweden from Copenhagen by boat, enjoying a smorgasbord of assorted hors d'oeuvres galore. Two American soldiers were stuffing themselves as if food were going out of sight. Hathaway kept trying to get their eye. Once she got their attention, perhaps a friendly conversation would develop and she would get a change to show off her knowledge about the customers of Scandinavian people. Having been a University of Minnesota graduate, she had been exposed to the ethnic group in Minnesota. No, the young men ignored her. After the hours of the hors d'oeuvres were over, then came the hot dishes of huge pork chops, potatoes, vegetables, and hot bread. The Americans were sick to think they gorged themselves and now could not eat another morsel of food!

That's when Hathaway had the last laugh. When they approached her and asked, "Have you been here before?" Hathaway answered, "Yes." "Then, why didn't you tell us about the food and their custom?" Hathaway said, "I tried to get your attention but you ignored me." I said to myself, "To hell with the poor ignoramuses."

LH had chosen to stay in Copenhagen so Hathaway had gone alone. She had an opportunity to meet a few of the relatives of one of her instructors while attending the University of Minnesota. She had an opportunity also to visit the church which contained one of the beams from one of the churches which Christ used in an Israel church centuries ago. The post was in the middle of the church in order to help hold up the roof. Down from the church was a castle that had been built centuries ago. The castle had four towers. There had been four daughters in the royal family. Each had her own tower. Hathaway has beautiful slides of this castle and other places of interest.

During the interim between vacations with LH, Hathaway, with other Army wives, took short trips to the castles and Oktoberfest. They would pool gasoline ration stamps, pack picnic baskets of foods, obtain rooms on Army bases in their guest houses. They would join tourist groups, leave them for lunch, return to their rooms to eat from the picnic baskets and regroup with the tourists. They attempted to create a picture of rich tourists traveling in Europe. One of the wives had to take her five-year old son along. He ended up sleeping between his mother and Hathaway and had to have all of the pillows. He was taken to se the Ice Follies at the NCO Club that was really swanky with tier-type settings. For dinner they decided they would order chicken. Hathaway liked the gristle of the chicken and at home, Tony never would give her the gristle. This particular night, with other guests at their table, Tony held the gristle up in the air and said, "Here, Hathaway!" People around gazed in awe. Hathaway, trying to look sophisticated, was really brought down. This little five-year old grew up to be a great football player. He was a card! At five. The German maid had taught him German and he would fuss with his mother in German which she did not understand and refused to learn. One day Hathaway had to punish him for his mother. By the time the ordeal was over, Hathaway had to go home and to bed. She never tackled Tony again!

It was in Oberammergau that the Passion Play was developed. Hathaway and friends visited the city. They learned the background of why the Play was done regularly.

Ships were crossing the Mediterranean Sea to reach other countries in order to find condiments and spices to preserve foods. Rats traveled on these ships, consequently the bubonic plague ran rampant in all of Europe: towns were wiped out. It was called the Black Death.

When the plague hit Oberammergau and practically wiped out the town, the people prayed to God to spare their town and not let any more of their people die. If he granted their wish, they would pay tribute by doing the crucifixion and resurrection of Christ every year. Their wish was granted. The time was later changed to every ten years. People from all over the world attend. The actors and actresses must live in the village and become proficient in the acting of their parts, as well as get to know the village people.

This play can be seen in several cities in the United States. The first was developed in the Black Hills of Dakota.

The first laws in Public Health began with the laws of quarantine of ships after the plague in 1600.

Hathaway and Tony's family again made a tour of Oberammergau, the town that began the passion plays after the bubonic plague in 1600. The play was not in session at the time but one could visit the wood carving shops, the amphitheater and props used in the plays. Nearby was the castle of gold ornaments built by Mad King Ludwig. Close by was the Starn River where he was supposed to have committed suicide.

This was the area where Hathaway and tourist groups stopped for coffee and tea at a quaint little coffee ship. It was customary for coffee and tea to be served on small silver platters. The German waitress brought coffee to all of the White Americans on the traditional silver platter, but to Hathaway she served only a cup and saucer, then with her hands, proceeded to take the sugar cubes out of the bowl and place them by Hathaway's cup. Hathaway waited until she completed her task, then in German told her to take it all back; that she never ate anything from a person's hands. She returned it to the kitchen, then served Hathaway as she had served the white tourists.

Those seated around Hathaway asked where she had learned German. They did not speak it but by the waitress returning with the correct way to treat a customer, they understood what Hathaway must have said to her. Hathaway smoked a cigarette, dumped it into the cup of coffee and walked out with the others. No tip and no pay for the coffee.

Side trips were made to Salzburg, Austria. Mozart's birthplace was very quaint. She toured his home and saw the small piano on which he composed his first works at age 5. Also visited were salt mines and catacombs used by the Christians during the Renaissance Period.

In Switzerland, Hathaway and LH went to attend one of their Army buddy's wedding in St. Galines. Their social life centered around gatherings in homes, playing bridge, dinner dances, pot luck suppers and old fashioned get-togethers. Hathaway met old acquaintances and schoolmates she had not seen since elementary school days twenty-five years before.

Hathaway's German family would get meats for her at their butcher. Soon she would have chitterling suppers for all of her White and Black friends. They all began to buy them from the German butcher. At that time the comissary did not carry them.

Hathaway was in the Reserve Army Nurse Corps. Although the whole Army was still segregated, Hathaway was allowed to attend the white reserve officers' meeting and affairs in Frankfurt, Germany. The formal dinner dances were fantastic. The only way any blacks could attend was through an invitation from Hathaway, the only Black member.

Several of the black officers' wives had acted very nasty toward Hathaway when they found out that they had been playing bridge with a non-commissioned officer's wife and they attempted to break up the bridge club. They had no idea the club members were Hathaway's sorors. When it came time for the formal officer's dinner dance, they begged Hathaway for invitations. Hathaway let them stand by for one hour before time of the affair, then she issued them an invitation. What these rank conscious people did not know was that LH was an officer during WW II and upon discharge, he entered college. Later when he decided to make the Army a career, time had expired for return to his officer's rank. Therefore, he re-enlisted as a sergeant. His commanding officer in Germany wanted him to sign specific forms and once again become an officer. LH was not interested.

The commanding officer a West Point Graduate contacted Hathaway and between the two they planned to make LH drunk, then get him to sign the form to have his officer's rank restored regardless of the time limit. LH sobered immediately and refused to sign the form. He had the last laugh. His commanding officer was very disappointed. He stated LH's IQ was borderline genius and the Army could most certainly use such a highly intelligent person.

Hathaway received her twenty-seventh year Red Cross pin and was honored with a fabulous bon voyage party before she and LH left for a Stateside assignment. The Red Cross invited Colonel Feldman to the affair.

Colonel Feldman, was the one person who had told the German and American club members he did not want a Negro ever to attend the club's conventions. That caused a division in the club. Many of the Germans who liked Hathaway left the club.

When he attended the Red Cross party that was a farewell party for Hathaway, he gave a letter of commendation and thanks for the "first of its kind Health Services to Dependent Families in Europe." "God takes care of babies and fools." "What goes around comes around." This was one satisfaction Hathaway has experienced throughout life. Later the Red Cross had Hathaway's contribution written in the Directory of International Biography, London, England, 1968.

Many farewell parties were given with gayety but became very sad in 1956 when LH received orders to report to Ft. Benning, Georgia. Hathaway was not interested in returning to the United States at that point. Life in Germany had been educational with all the opportunities to visit all over Europe - very stimulating and fun with excitement. Conditions for Blacks in the South were improving but slowly. Accommodations traveling through the South were a dreaded expectation.

After a short furlough in each of their homes, Hathaway and LH drove to his assignment in Georgia. They began to settle in their new surroundings and became acquainted with new friends,. They began adjusting to the limitations of the South.

Hathaway began working in one of the Catholic Hospitals. Everything was separate in this hospital. The white nurses were addressed as Mrs. or Miss. The blacks were addressed as Nurse Brown, etc. One of Hathaway's friends from an Army family in Germany was sent to Georgia. She and Hathaway ended up working at the same hospital. Between the two, they began to confuse the nuns by addressing each other as Mrs. instead of Nurse Green, etc. The doctors were very insulting to the black nurses. On an occasion when applying traction with weights to a patient, a doctor cursed Hathaway because she refused to apply the weights for him. She returned the insults, took off her cap and immediately left the hospital informing the nuns to keep the salary as a donation because she would never return to their hospital.

Since there were no vacancies on the Public Health Nursing staff in Georgia, Hathaway volunteered to assist in the clinic. In the meantime she sought employment at the Veterans Administration Hospital in Tuskegee, only to be told by a big fat director of nursing, Ms. Moody, that she was too fat to be hired and there she was herself, big and fat. Hathaway told her that she should look in the mirror. Later, when an epidemic of a parasitic disease developed, the chief nurse called for Hathaway to come in and handle the special cases. Hathaway called the Public Health Department to state that she would not be available for the volunteer service. The director was shocked by the call stating that no one had ever let her know in advance when they could not keep an appointment to do volunteer work. This phone call was very profitable later when Hathaway began teaching and needed an agency for her students to affiliate. This director offered her agency to Hathaway and later wanted her to instruct her student nurses, both black and white. Never like this had this ever happened in Georgia.

While Hathaway was specializing at the Veterans Administration, rumors circulated that she was a representative or spy from the Pentagon so the chief nurse found a job for her in no time. A couple of weeks later, the dean of the School of Nursing at the local university in the area contacted Hathaway and offered a position at the university as Associate Professor. She was to teach Public Health Nursing. The accreditation for the school was being held up until a well-developed public health program was established for the student nurses. Another professor who graduated from the St. Louis School of Nursing was hired to teach obstetrics.

Hathaway loved teaching. Therefore she accepted the position and immediately began to develop a Public Health Nursing Program exactly as she had experienced it as a student at the University of Minnesota School of Public Health.

She did a survey of the economic, political and recreational areas. The area had a payroll of a half-million dollars a month between the two facilities in the area. There were no recreational areas. There was apparent friction between the employees of the two facilities.

Usually a public health program for students consist of lectures, then practical application of principles in a public health agency in a community. At that time segregation prevented black students from affiliating in the Southern Public Health Agencies.

Hathaway had to develop programs for practical application. The plans included home visits referred by the physicians in the area, an extensive school health program that would require students to develop and teach health classes in the schools. They would participate in a federally funded research project which was coordinated with obstetric-laboratory and dietary departments. "Physical reactions of Pregnant women who ate starch, clay, red dirt, or newspapers" were observed. Stool specimens were collected for laboratory study to determine if any of the chemicals had been assimilated. The impact of the psychological theory was integrated in the study.

Hathaway scheduled consultants and physicians to lecture on each of the categories of the equipment in order to correlate its usage in relationship to anatomy and physiology and treatment given when necessary.

The director of the Public Health Department in Georgia did allow Hathaway to bring groups for one day observations. Later the director contacted the dean of the school of nursing and offered the agency as a department for practical application providing that Hathaway would be the instructor and also teach their students, white and black ones, principles of public health nursing. The offer was rejected by the acting Dean at the School of Nursing at Tuskegee.

The president gave Hathaway's department an unlimited budget. She contacted her instructors at the University of Minnesota and obtained material, pamphlets, addresses to purchase equipment and methods to develop a tutorial program campus-wide.

The tutorial program was developed after a faculty meeting with the President present. The committee for student evaluation proposed a different method to be used in evaluating students. Hathaway asked if there were methods to evaluate the faculty's teaching because she had found many of her senior students lacking in knowledge that should have been taught prior to public health classes. For example, they did not know the Federal Government was in Washington, D.C., or the number of senators and representatives, the Public Health Agency in a community involves funds from Federal, State, and local governments. Also, English and sentence structure in the required project papers from her students were horrible - single subjects with plural verbs and vice versa. A Ph.D professor became very indignant by stating that he was not an English instructor. Hathaway asked how did he comprehend the content if the English were incorrect and that he should address all issues of written reports with his students if he wanted to help them. This same professor questioned the need for tutorial services at an undergraduate level; he had never heard of such at that level. Hathaway stated some students at all levels except Ph.D (she hoped not) needed tutorial services. The President asked Hathaway to work with the English department to help develop tutorial services.

Hathaway was well aware of the benefits of a tutorial program. Her experience - When she returned to the University of Minnesota, after eight years, her counselor, on the basis of past scholastic ratings, assigned Hathaway to many science courses. The Zoology class was overloaded with students and the way to eliminate students was by written examination within a month.

Hathaway flunked the examination. The advisor and Dean of Public Health Nursing would not allow her and a classmate to be dropped from the class. Within a matter of ten minutes, a tutor had been assigned to Hathaway.

She purchased screening equipment, an audiometer, Massachusetts vision kit, Wood's lamp to diagnose ringworm on the scalp. Medication for treatment was furnished by the university and, one of the stores in the community ordered white sailor caps for all the students to wear and this eliminated embarrassment to students who were positive since all students wore the caps and no one knew positives from negatives.

Hathaway scheduled consultants and physicians to lecture on each of the categories of the equipment in order to correlate its usage in relationship to anatomy and physiology and treatment given when necessary. In order to enlighten the public, Hathaway wrote health education articles weekly for the local paper.

Audio visual material was obtained from the Reserve Officer's Training Corps, maps and slides of various diseases worldwide. Hathaway used her slides from Oberammagau about the bubonic plague that led to the development of the Passion Play. Students were taken on tours of water purification plants and other environmental areas.

Adult classes were developed for those parents who would be volunteer aides to participate in screening the school children. Standing orders for school nurses were obtained and permission forms had to be signed by parents.

Conferences were held with the school principals to obtain contracts that would allow the student nurses to affiliate in their schools for school nurse experience. Only one principal hesitated in allowing the students in her school. She feared the superintendent, who was white, would think she was not doing her job of teaching by allowing time to be used in screening.

Hathaway became irate and asked her where on earth had she obtained a degree and not know that mental and physical well-being was necessary and most important for learning to take place; that the superintendent could obtain medical care any time he needed, but did the black children have these privileges? She finally gave in.

The same superintendent called the university president and asked if Hathaway and her student would cross county lines to check the other students, that he had wished for this kind of school service for the black children. All told, the students screened over 3,000 school children. The Lions Club, for the first time in history in that area, donated glasses immediately when Hathaway made the contact for help. One professor tried to tell her that the Lions Club did not donate to blacks.

Another school was without running water. There were no facilities to wash hands after using the outside flush-type toilets and no drinking water. The students would bring jars of drinking water from home. They and the teachers would forget to bring fresh water daily, consequently they were drinking water from several days to weeks old. County issued food was stored in the rat infested kitchen and the refrigerator was rancid. No hot lunches, therefore most the children had no food after breakfast at home until they returned in the evening.

Hathaway and her students took hand washing equipment and taught the young students the process with pitchers and basins. Personal and oral hygiene were included in the teaching. The principal had the kitchen cleaned, new shelves installed and the room painted. Parents volunteered their time and developed a hot lunch program with the county food that had been sent for hot lunches.

Hathaway took LH with her to the Parent-Teachers Association meeting and demanded that the parent go to the County Building to obtain equipment and install running water in that school. Over Thanksgiving holiday, the parents installed the pipes, pump, etc.

There were no recreation facilities for adults or children in this town. One could hardly believe such with an income of over a half a million dollars a month. Once agriculture was discontinued, the land had become covered with weeds. Hathaway began asking the parents to develop money rasing projects to buy recreational equipment. Some of the parents because indignant and told her that, when their children reached a certain age, they were sent North to schools where all types of recreation were available. Those parents who were interested had cookouts, sold dinners, etc., to develop some type of recreational activities. In a two-year period, they had over $1,300 toward the project. Thirty years later, Hathaway visited the place. Apparently the parents gave up because the situation remained the same - still no recreational facilities.

One Georgia paper had written that blacks were inferior intellectually. At that time many black student nurses were failing State Board Exams the first time around. Hathaway told her students that such an editorial should make them want to make a liar and fool of the editor, besides they had a brain that could be used intelligently. Hathaway and her co-worker from St. Louis demanded excellence. They held tutorial classes and review sessions. Hathaway used the CIA method in teaching: her students must Correlate, Integrate and Associate all subjects. The two instructors' method paid off. That year the majority of the students made the highest scores possible on the State Board Examinations. The accreditation inspectors were very pleased with Hathaway's Student Public Health Program and the school received its accreditation.

This was a new experience for Hathaway. She was used to the caste system in the black race. In fact, the system has been around since the beginning of time. But she was not accustomed to some teachers short-changing students as she observed in this town. Most of her formative years of learning was from black teachers and, in elementary and secondary schools, her mentor had cared and demanded only the best from all of her students. The instructors at the University of Minnesota had required excellence. To come to this small town, supposedly populated with predominately educated people and encounter such attitudes of blacks against blacks, was more than she could tolerate. During the day she used to go into the Episcopal church to sit and cry. LH suggested she give up the job. Those people were too set in their ways to care about a change.

At one of the PTA meetings in the Campus Elementary School, Hathaway attempted to explain that from previous experiences, she had found ring worm of the scalp more prevalent in black children and head lice more prevalent in white children. One of the mulatto PhD professors asked if she had found ringworm more prevalent in the darker skinned children than the lighter ones. Hathaway said under breath, "Oh God, here is another one of those sons . . . she had encountered during her growing up in Southern Illinois." Hathaway let one of the mulatto outstanding physician and surgeon answer the questions. The physician let him have it. The physician became an instructor at the integrated Emory University in Atlanta.

Hathaway discussed the problem of insufficient school buses. She had observed students standing up to the edge of the dashboard. Should the driver stop suddenly, many students could be injured. Since these children were from the indigent areas, would the professional people contact the Board of Education and demand more busses? Several parents stated that their children did not have to ride the busses because they drove their children to school. No one ever came forward to change the situation.

This was the home town of the secretary Hathaway had met at the VA Hospital in Michigan. Her family welcomed Hathaway as part of their family. LH would pull little Richie in his wagon all around the neighborhood. This little boy grew up to be an outstanding singer.

Three years later, LH was assigned as Military Science Instructor at a university in Florida. Hathaway commuted weekends. When she took the busses, it was pure hell. All blacks had to ride in the back of the bus. The colored bathrooms were absolutely filthy and the waiting rooms were filled with trash. Hathaway felt the blacks should have had some pride and not litter their waiting room. One weekend the fumes in the back of the bus caused Hathaway to become nauseated with severe diarrhea. By the time she arrived in Alabama, she had discarded all of her clothing except dress and trench coat. Hathaway began always to sit in the middle of the bus. The driver only asked her one time to move back. This she refused to do. He did not make an issue and left her.

When LH moved to Florida as a Military Science instructor, Hathaway moved into the Faculty Dormitory until her contract ended with the university there in Alabama. Hathaway was exposed to operas at Forest Park in St. Louis, Missouri, where she had worked as a maid to obtain tuition for nurse's training. The maid's day off was every Thursday and she would go to the park. Later during the military assignment in Germany, her German instructor required opera membership. She had not studied music. In order to make her nights productive and have some knowledge of the opera music, Hathaway enrolled in Music History and Appreciation night classes at Tuskegee University. Other nights were spent becoming a Scrabble champion with her co-worker who later moved to New York.

After three and half years teaching at the University in Alabama, Hathaway ended the commuting by accepting an appointment as Assistant Professor in the School of Nursing at Florida University. Hathaway had no idea what was awaiting her in this new assignment at this university and in the community. She was in for a rude awakening. She would have continued to teach in Georgie if the Acting Dean had accepted the Georgia Public Health Department's request.

The homes were infested with roaches. The community people stated the climate was conducive to growth and infestation of roaches in the homes. Hathaway informed them that roaches bred in dirty kept homes and especially when food was around in the kitchens. The pest control people came and sprayed the home; painters went through the house, all plumber areas were checked for entrance of roaches and replacements made where needed. Once the house was free of roaches, the Army delivered the furniture from their storage. Never was a roach found in Hathaway's home.

The next morning Hathaway met with the Dean of Nursing and was given her assignment as Public Health instructor. Hathaway immediately began preparation of her class outline. Her visit to the library was most disappointing because the books needed in the program were outdated by fourteen years. She requested updated books immediately before she would even begin the classes. Books were flown in as requested.

In order to implement instructions, Hathaway contacted the City Health Department. She asked to borrow equipment for testing hearing, vision, ringworm and light lamps for checking the lighting system in the classrooms. The director informed her that the university should have its own equipment. Hathaway informed him that his department was supported with state funds the same as the university, therefore the equipment was supposed to be exchanged between the two facilities and, if necessary, she would call the State Department. The director stated the equipment would be delivered the next day accompanied with orders to assist her. He apologized by saying no one had ever before requested the equipment.

Hathaway, as a delegate from the university, attended the National Public Health Association Convention in St. Louis, Mo. Upon returning, her report was classified as outstanding and a few of the staff members accepted implementation of several resolutions from the Convention. The State Public Health representatives were very enthusiastic and were quite anxious to integrate the suggestions.

Next on the agenda was for Hathaway to meet with the State Public Health staff in order to outline the schedule for practical application in field training assignments. Hathaway arrived at the meeting with an outline of experiences she expected the students to receive during the semester. The State Administrators were very impressed and stated it seemed as if Hathaway's type of program correlated with their objectives and procedures just fine; that they had planned to discontinue their affiliations but with such a projected program, they would reconsider and become involved again. A few of the staff and Hathaway had graduated from the same university, consequently they approached this program with the same philosophy - "Develop a well informed and capable student who can function in any situation." The trend in the South was to address all Negro nurses as Nurse Smith and not Mrs. Smith. After Hathaway's conference and development of affiliating with the State Department, the department wrote a newspaper article of the scheduled program in the area of Florida and, as a shock to the State of Florida, the newspaper article set a precedent throughout by addressing Hathaway as "Mrs." instead of their steadfast rule to address Negro nurses as "Nurse" and never "Mrs." Hathaway had experienced such at the Catholic Hospital in Georgia where she and a white colleague confused the nuns by addressing each other as "Mrs." Hathaway did not have it any easier than her other position; in fact, the situations at the university were much more difficult.

At one of the ROTC campus formal affairs, the President of the University introduced himself to Hathaway and said, "I am happy to meet you. I hear that you are a dynamic person. We're please to have you on the faculty." Hathaway said, "Thanks" and under her breath she wanted to ask him why in the hell he had issued an old beat up used university owned car, for transportation with the students. In order to start the car, one had to give it a push down the hill. When it rained, one had to place a umbrella under the dashboard. The state trooper stopped her on the highway and asked where had she gotten such an old dilapidated car and why she had not removed the university emblem. He was shocked when Hathaway told him that she was one of the instructors from the university and the car had been issued to use in her work as Public Health Nurse when she made home visits. He shook his head, tore up the traffic ticket and drove off. The students really laughed.

Instructions consisted of Correlation Integration and Association. Slides of the little city of Oberrammergau, Germany, were shown. This city developed the Passion Play that is now shown in various cities in America. The students were requested to see this play in their state-Wake Florida. Visits for the first time were made to facilities that would broaden the students' knowledge. State and local health departments were contacted for loan of equipment needed to supplement the classroom lectures. Hathaway developed an exchange of professional magazines with the only White University School of Nursing.

Projects, newspaper articles and required reading material had to be well written with correct sentence structure and spelling. Public Health uniforms had to be worn when on duty. The students resented these and other requirements; they felt the instructor was too strict. This was the first time students had been assigned to three small communities where white and black had not seen or met professional student nurses, therefore Hathaway saw to their portraying a professional image. Frequent conferences were held to inform each student of her good points, weak areas and methods of improvement. The Board of Education was quite happy to have student school nurses in their schools. This had never happened before. They were elated to have nursing care in the homes.

The students resented Hathaway's requirements. They were to wear complete Public Health type uniforms, not to visit bars to drink; not to chew gum while on duty. One student gave her a required newspaper report that was awesome!! Hathaway told the student that such a report would have been on the radio and headlines in the paper and asked what paper carried the story. The student stated that she made up the story just to find out what Hathaway would say since she seemed to know everything. The student apologized for lying.

Another student wrote a required project paper on an Allied Health Personnel. She chose to write about an engineer. In her paper, the engineer finished high school and immediately became an engineer with the Health Department. Hathaway discussed the content and advised her that a person must obtain a degree in Engineering before being hired. The student did not accept Hathaway's advice and grade, therefore she asked one of the Public Health officers read and upgrade it over Hathaway's grade. He called a meeting with the student and Hathaway in order to clear up the problem by telling the student that her instructor was absolutely correct in her remarks and grade on the paper. The student was very embarrassed and apologized to Hathaway.

The students in Florida were not too different from the students at the Alabama University. They felt Hathaway was too strict and had asked the dean there to give them an extra day off duty to have more time since Hathaway was too demanding. The dean would not interfer with Hathaway's schedule. One of the other instructors and Hathaway tutored the Alabama students since the paper had stated they were slow Negroes. These students made a lie of the report and scored exceptionally high on the state board exam. Two of the graduate students were the first to be admitted to all white Emory University. This made national news.

The campus was wild. Instructor and student relationships were very questionable; gossip of sexually transmitted disease was rampant. Contributions were collected from all faculty members to purchase gifts for the President and family for every occasion: birthdays, anniversaries, summer vacation trips and even trips to Europe. The roster was checked and non contributors' contracts were not renewed. When Hathaway was approached, she advised the collector that she did not have to pay for assurance of a job; that when she studied to become a professional person, she made sure to become one of the best in her field and she would never crawl for anything in this life.

Apparently Hathaway was too outspoken, too strict and demanding of excellency from her students, because they began to complain to the Alumni that Hathaway was making derogatory remarks about the university; that her landlord was about to evict her because a white man came calling. What the students and landlord did not know until later was that the white man was a Negro doctor who practiced in Florida and was Hathaway's instructor when she was a student nurse and when he heard that she was in the area, he had come to visit. When Hathaway returned from a weekend at home, the landlord had packed her things for eviction. It was surprising how little these people knew about the NAACP activities in the areas. This Negro doctor and family were the leaders who had integrated the Florida beaches, jobs in the post office and community housing in most of the East Coast and Ft. Lauderdale.

Many week ends, the Commanding Officer of the ROTC Unit at the University and Hathaway would play scrabble without interruptions. His wife and LH would prepare the food and serve the two. Hathaway bought the only very large *Webster's Dictionary* for reference when challenged. "*Q* without *U*" was Hathaway's specialty in spelling. He was shocked when it was in the dictionary.

Hathaway had begun to wonder if this job was really what

she wanted. She began to reminisce. When she was teaching in Alabama, she was quite concerned about the apparent diluted education for Negro students in the South. Now all of this bickering. Her mentor from her home had visited her classroom to evaluate Hathaway's methods of teaching. She was quite pleased.

Thank God for the sisterly love that existed in the Georgia sorority and later the Florida chapter. They counteracted the stress-anxiety syndromes. the Georgia chapter gave Hathaway a beautiful sterling silver pendulum with the crest of the sorority.

On long weekends, Hathaway and LH would explore Florida and surrounding states. They would take their friends' children on many of these jaunts: exploring Silver Springs in glass bottom boats; Marineland Zoo and swimming in the Gulf of Mexico. One trip to the Bahamas was enough for a lifetime. The life style there was severe-only rich or poor, no in-between.

Hathaway was ready to chuck the job and stay at home anyway because women in the community would find out if the wives were away, and would invite themselves into the homes for party time. LH had an affair with one of the secretaries that led to a very unpleasant experience. It was only six years since his last episode in Maryland - Problems - Problems!! The first episode in Maryland was supposed to release Hathaway of her marriage vows in order to pursue her dreams to the top of the ladder in the nursing field. They were separated until she finished her contract at the VA Hospital. Now this second episode in Florida once again separated them until the contract ended in Alabama. What's the deal? Was there really any love in this marriage? It seemed as if every occasion when jobs called for separation, trouble began. When assigned overseas, then it might be understandable if one dates a person, but not if separation is stateside.

Hathaway would soon make a decision if she would terminate this marriage and return to Templeton whom she should have kept her promise to marry in the beginning before going overseas as an Army nurse.

The President listened to the Alumni's complaints and made the mistake of calling Hathaway back to the campus and sent a relief. He waited three days after the recall before he had a conference. The State Department became outraged over the interruption of a program that they stated was the best ever since they had become involved in the training of students, therefore, they wanted an explanation immediately.

The State Public Health Department contacted Hathaway and offered her a position on the staff; also that it had a stipend for a student to obtain a Master's Degree in Public Health Nursing at the University of Michigan in Ann Arbor, the department asked would she be interested and that the contract would expect the recipient to work at least two years with the Department. The offer was tempting, but Hathaway had never become obligated to anyone but her mentor and too, she had her fill of the south's racial principles. And yet, by the same token, what better way to get a Master's Degree in Public Health Nursing without having to pay? She needed to obtain three documents, high school diploma, nurses' training diploma and the university transcript. Hathaway contacted the three places. The high school sent a transcript with incorrect name and grades, subjects listed that were not even offered when she attended and grades in those subjects would have classified her as a moron. Such a grade point average would not have allowed her to enter nurses' training. When she contacted them about the mistakes, the answer was that a fire or flood had destroyed some students' records. What a lie!

The Director of the School of Nursing was taking too long in responding to the request because the university contacted Hathaway and requested that she obtain the material immediately if she wished to be considered. Again Hathaway wrote and stated that since she did not send the transcript, she would obtain papers from the Administrators at the Missouri State Education Department. In retaliation, the Director sent Hathaway an insulting answer with the State Department address in the event she cared to write them. The transcript she sent to the University of Michigan was not accurate. The grades had been changed because Hathaway had a high point average during her training. She was elected President of the whole student body and received honors as the most outstanding student and went on to win the award from Mrs. Mabel Keaton Staupers RN, Author of "No Time For Prejudice." The award was a beautiful hand printed silk blouse.

When Hathaway left home for school and the Army, all of

her papers were supposed to be in her mother's trunk. Some years later she received her high school diploma from her mentor. Whatever happened to her other school grades, etc., she had no idea. Her mentor kept up with her grades and was quite pleased with them during Hathaway's nurses' training. She went so far as to enlighten the hometown people of Hathaway's progress in Nurses' Training.

Hathaway's transcript from the University of Minnesota where she had obtained her B.S. Degree with certificate in Public Health Nursing had three grades of "D" in three subjects the first semester. With the aid of tutors, she brought her grade point up to a B average by graduation. Combination of the three transcripts disqualified her for the stipend. It didn't hurt too badly because she did not wish to be obligated to the State of Florida at that time anyway. She wanted to get as far away as possible after all she had gone through. Not only problems on the job but treacherous remarks from some of the community women because of facial hair. The rumor had begun to circulate that Hathaway must be a lesbian. When a supposedly friend told her, Hathaway told her that if they knew her true record, they might classify her as a nymphomaniac!

Under a photo taken in Florida, she wrote: "Leaving the South and the only way I shall ever return is by a glacier period and my coffin is washed south.

When Hathaway walked into the President's office, she opened her briefcase and laid out the whole program. The President was surprised, stated he had no idea that the Public Health Nursing program contained such minute details and was so well organized. He stated that someone must have been jealous of her program, and the excellent progress, and would she reconsider and return to the field in Northern Florida. He had been contacted by the State Department and they wanted Hathaway to be reinstated in the position. Hathaway told him that she was so cocky in her field that if necessary she would challenge the Secretary of Health, Education and Welfare when it came to Public Health Principles and teaching of same, therefore she would not teach another class on his campus. He asked Hathaway to talk with the Dean of Students in order for him to begin an investigation of who started such rumors that caused him to act so hastily. Hathaway told him that as president he had the privilege to follow up on any adverse situation on his campus, but he should have had a conference with her first before such drastic actions, and if she could not justify the accusations, then he could have made his move with a replacement. Hathaway promised him that she would only talk to the Dean.

When Hathaway went in to talk with Dean Ephiman, he told her that she brought trouble to the campus by being the first instructor to take the students on field trips to water purification plants, health problem sites in the community, having consultants and agencies to display health equipment, that she had recently purchased books before she started her classes, etc. What she should have done as a new faculty member was to wait until she was accepted by the older faculty members, then she could branch out with her new ideas and methods. Hathaway became very angry and said, "To hell with you, man. You are wasting my time to even suggest that I should have waited for faculty acceptance before teaching the students a well-developed program; I am not interested in your damn theory!" The Dean jumped up and said, "That's bad language!" Hathaway said, "Again, to hell with you, stupid fool! walked out and slammed the door behind her.

The people became frightened and rather than have Hathaway come to the office for her monthly salary, they had LH pick up her check. Faculty members would cross the street if they were about to meet Hathaway for fear they would lose their jobs should someone report that they were seen talking to her. Incidentally, Hathaway was paid her salary monthly and she refused to teach another class.

Hathaway bought sewing books, materials and taught herself how to sew. She had a philosophy that if a person could read then she should be able to operate a sewing machine. She used a lot of material until she became a fairly good seamstress. As she sewed, her mind began to reflect over all the experiences she had encountered in the South in such a short time: the many super egotistical people responsible for the education of black student nurses according to Hathaway's evaluation, were not in tune with update principles. The President of this University returned $700,000 to the State Educational Fund. Yet, the students were risking their lives to manually close the auditorium draperies that were ragged and on broken drapery rods; the library void of late edition books in all disciplines. The experiences were disgusting. There was not acceptable excuse for shortchanging the students.

LH and Hathaway took a trip to a New York to see "Members of the Wedding;" any excuse to get away from so much campus confusion and anxiety. Too, this visit was an opportunity for Hathaway to visit an ex co-worker at the Alabama University. She had been the co-worker who had helped to tutor the students and when they took the State Board Examination, many of them went to the very top of the scores. This was very rewarding for her and Hathaway's efforts.

Hathaway had LH and Templeton to visit over dinner at the co-worker's home. The two had not met since Hathaway left for overseas assignment during WW II. Hathaway and Lt. Templeton were in the process of getting married but the overseas assignment took priority. When the troops gathered at the train station, LH told Lt. Templeton that he would look after Hathaway, therefore do not worry. The Lt. thanked him.

When Templeton came to Hathaway's rescue in Maryland, he refused to see LH. Hathaway felt it was about time to clear the air. Was it ever a mistake! The two became intoxicated and began to discuss their experiences with Hathaway when they dated her. Hathaway, a non-alcoholic began to drink also. It ended up with all three "high as a kite!" When it came time to return to Florida, Hathaway wanted to remain in New York near Templeton to renew their relationship. LH insisted that Hathaway accompany him back to Florida.

Once back in Florida, LH and Hathaway had heated arguments. Hathaway wanted to end the marriage and return to New York. She recalled the Maryland episode and later in Florida, the secretary affair. LH told Hathaway that if she wanted to return to New York, do it on a temporary basis and if she wished to come back to Florida, he would be waiting. During this controversy, LH received his Korean assignment. His Commanding Officer wanted to have the orders rescinded, but LH did not wish this and stated he would have to leave in order to get his crazy wife out of Florida.

Preparations to move went into gear immediately; once again furniture was back in Army storage. Hathaway's sorority sisters had farewell affairs. The community neighbors who were secure in their jobs on the campus came by with farewell gifts. The problem of the return to New York was placed on hold. She called Templeton and told him of the conversation with LH and that she would contact him later. LH and Hathaway began the drive to West Coast. While enroute, they encountered segregation: no bathrooms for Negroes at the gas stations. There was a coffee can and toilet paper in the car. Hathaway would use the can, then throw the urine and paper on the gas pump. She almost wrecked the car by throwing out the can as she drove across the Arizona border. She no longer needed the can. Hathaway had suggested that they speak only German, then the whites would serve them. He refused to do this.

Hathaway had written several Public Health Agencies on the West Coast. All had responded with an appointment date for interviews. A doctor at the Florida Public Health Agency, in response to these agencies' requests for references, had written that they had better employ Hathaway immediately before any other agency contacted her, if only she had considered his offer to join his staff.

The scenery across the South was beautiful. No time was wasted in Mississippi, only for gas, and out like lightning; many stops for short visits with army families who had retired and were living in Houston, Texas, Baton Rouge and new Orleans. They continued on to White Sands, New Mexico, for a week with friends, then the desert areas through Arizona and on into Los Angeles, California.

WEST COAST

CALIFORNIA

Before leaving Florida for the West Coast, Hathaway wrote to several Public Health Departments on the Coast for a job assignment. Each department upon receiving her resume became quite anxious to have her on the staff. The Director of the Florida Public Health Department advised that they hurry before another agency hired her since the Florida Dept. was not successful in keeping her in Florida.

Santa Ana and San Bernardino Public Health Departments each had offered Hathaway a position on their staff. She had to go to San Bernardino for a written examination. When Hathaway drove from L.A. to S.B., the trip on the expressway was very confusing and created a very nervous reaction before taking the exam. However, she passed the exam and was expected to report for work in two weeks.

In the two week period before LH left for assignment in Korea, he and Hathaway visited classmates and army buddies. Hathaway's boyfriend during her college days heard that she was in L.A. He immediately came to visit and invited her and LH to his home to meet his family and for Hathaway to again visit his mother, who had to move in with him, and present of his family. He took Hathaway into the children's bedroom to see the newborn. As they talked, he attempted to kiss Hathaway, not aware that the mirror in the room revealed into the living room his actions. LH saw this. LH asked Hathaway not to become again involved with the guy. She began to think about the episodes involving the past and the stress involved in commuting to her job from L.A. to San Bernardino. Hathaway decided to leave the area. Now would be timely to visit a classmate in San Francisco and to take a trip to Hawaii to decide on divorcing LH.

The two had discussed the divorce prior to their leaving Florida. LH had suggested that she go for a trial visit to New York where Templeton was living and if she decided not to divorce him, he would be waiting for her to come back to continue their marriage.

LH and Hathaway moved into a classmate's home with two extra rooms. She called Templeton in New York and gave him her plans; that she would visit friends in Hawaii to think over the divorce and, upon her return, she would call him as to the verdict.

Hathaway called an army family friend in Hawaii and made plans to visit. LH left for Korea and thought that the army troop plane would stop in Hawaii, which would give him an opportunity to have another visit with Hathaway. But the plane Hathaway was on had trouble, therefore the reunion trip was void. The army family now stationed in Hawaii had been stationed with LH and Hathaway in Hanau, Germany. The reunion was great.

Tours were made over the island. The first world mall was being built. The Punch Bowl was the cemetery for Army veterans. Its structure was outstanding. There were daily swimming sessions at Waikiki beach. One island where pineapples were grown had a very bad history, was classified as a slave area with primitive living conditions, no electricity, no outside toilets; people were treated as heathens with very low salaries.

The area where Hathaway's friend lived was well developed: beautiful homes, fashionable clothes and mumu dresses in various styles and colors, grass skirts used for dancing. The dancing show girls would meet every plane arrival and greet the passengers with dances. Of course Hathaway bought one of the grass skirts, enrolled in the dance classes and to this day continues to do the dance along with the belly dance.

Civilian and army wives had bridge clubs, tours of the islands and luncheons in their homes. A very congenial, friendly atmosphere existed between the families. Hathaway went for a month and ended spending three months. Many pictures were taken during this trip. They helped to reminisce.

Upon her return to San Francisco, just as Hathaway entered her home, the phone rang and it was Templeton calling from New York. He asked if she were going to get the divorce and come to him for marriage. Hathaway told him that she had decided not to go through a divorce at this time. He told her that he would marry the young lady who stated that her child was his son. He did not believe her, but since Hathaway had continued to refuse him, he would marry her. He died a year and a half after his marriage.

Hathaway settled in San Francisco and decided to do private duty nursing whenever she so desired. She enrolled in the University of San Francisco to begin work toward a Master's Degree in Education; played bridge with Sorority sisters and Deltas. The County Health Department heard that Hathaway was in the area, made contact and offered her a position on the staff. Hathaway and the director agreed on the salary which was conducive toward full time employment.

When Hathaway reported for duty, she noticed that the secretary was typing Hathaway's salary scale. She told the secretary to discontinue typing and call the director down to the office because the salary was not like the agreement. When the director arrived, she told Hathaway that when all references came in, her salary would be retroactive to the agreed amount; that so far, references showed her to have excellent expertise; to go have lunch and think about returning to work there because the department would love to have her on the staff. Hathaway told her that no way would she come to work at such a salary and if she wished to use her expertise, then pay the price...Good bye!

Hathaway told her bridge partners about the episode. She continued to share her experiences in Hawaii; how the visit at Pearl Harbor brought back memories of the episode involving the inductions of Negro nurses during the preparation for World War II. The Army Nurse Corps was established in 1901 and when preparations began for participants, the Surgeon General refused to accept Negro nurses into the corps. Mrs. Eleanor

Roosevelt, Mrs. Bethune McCloud and Mrs. Mable Staupers, President of the now defunct Negro Graduate Nurses Association, met with the Surgeon General and demanded that he admit Negro nurses into the Army Nurse Corps. He advised them that he would allow only forty-eight into the Corps. Twenty-four were sent to Fort Bragg, N.C. and twenty-four to Camp Livingston, La. This camp was very shortly closed and the nurses were dispersed to Fort Braggs and Fort Huachuca, Arizona. When Pearl Harbor was bombed, the Surgeon General and Red Cross Corps began to recruit all races; as many as possible.

The following week, Hathaway reported to the Private Duty Nurse office for an assignment. The director was happy to see her because she was disappointed at losing Hathaway to the Health Department, so she thought. Hathaway told her what had happened at the Health Department.

There was excellent rapport between Hathaway and the Private Duty Director. She typed all of Hathaway's college reports. A couple of weeks later when Hathaway reported for an assignment, she told the director that she had thought of attending the University full time because the private duty relief people were not too interested in giving excellent care to the patients; her relief had become very angry when Hathaway shaved a male patient; stated that she would not shave a patient. Hathaway told her to mind her own business since she had no feelings for the comfort of patients.

The next day, Hathaway was assigned to a critically ill infant. The infant expired. Hathaway had to take the infant to the morgue and as she walked and walked to find the morgue, rigormortis set in and the infant began to weigh a ton.

All of the above was just too much. When Hathaway went into the office to resign, the director greeted her with a message from the San Francisco Board of Education. She said that she was aware that Hathaway did not wish a permanent job, but the situation might change her mind, that the Board of Education needed a nurse with teaching credentials for one of its high schools, that the Board did not have too many Negroes employed and would she consider, Hathaway told her that she would think it over and called the Principal later that day. The Director stated,

"Good! Your appointment is at 2 p.m." She knew that Hathaway would break the barrier.

Hathaway kept the two o'clock appointment. The Principal and assistant greeted her. The Principal told her that he had interviewed three other nurses who did not impress him. Hathaway asked if his degree was PhD or M.D. He stated, PhD. Then why would he question the qualities of RNs? He immediately took Hathaway to the assigned quarters of the position. He stated the interview was most interesting and to please report to the Personnel office to apply for her salary. Hathaway was the only female Negro on the staff and there was only one male Negro on the athletic staff. The school had an enrollment of two-thousand students and a Disability School for the handicapped. It was the largest school in San Francisco.

When Hathaway attended her bridge sessions, one of the teachers asked, since she was a nurse, what was she doing at the Board of Education personnel office. Hathaway stated she had been offered a job at the high school but she did not really want a full time job; she did not state that she had accepted the position. Later that day, one of the women at the bridge party called the Principal; impersonated Hathaway by saying that since she did not qualify for the position to hire someone else. The principle of the school system where teachers were involved was to hire them as substitutes until a permanent position became available. The impersonator did not know that being a registered nurse with teaching credentials was the requirement for the job. The Principal called Hathaway and asked if she had followed up on going to the Personnel office and signed the payroll. When she told him that she had done so, he did not talk further.

Hathaway's assignment at the school was fascinating and challenging. Students would crowd the dispensary to cut classes. They were not aware that when Hathaway left the room, she adjusted the shade and could observe activity. Some of the students would get up and dance around the room. She would immediately return the perpetrators to class. One of the dancing students told her that he was very ill and might die if he returned to class. Hathaway told him if he died, his mortician would come for him, therefore return to his class. Another student was practicing football on the field next to the school. He fell in a hole in the yard. Hathaway applied first-aid and then called his parents to come for him. The stepfather stated his mother was at work and since he had for the first time begun to work on a new job, he could not come for the boy; have him to take a bus home. Hathaway advised the father that a bus ride with the injury would be detrimental. This conversation was recorded. The student had to take the bus home. The parents took the student to their doctor. He applied a cast. The parents began a suit of neglect against the school. When the Board of Education presented Hathaway's recording of the conversation, the lawyer dropped the case and the doctor immediately removed the two-day old cast from the student's leg. The teachers were shocked because they had never seen a fracture heal in two days. Hathaway had to explain the situation. The Board of Education was very appreciative of Hathaway's actions of recording the conversation with the parent.

The school had a "Future Nurses Club" that was attended by only female students. During this era, no male students were considered suitable to become nurses. If they attended such a club, they would be classified as "faggots." Hathaway wrote the National League of Nurses and was granted permission to develop a "Paramedic Club" to replace the Future Nurse Club. The attendance became terrific with students interested in becoming physicians, pharmacists, dentists, medical technicians, nurses, etc. The club continued for years after Hathaway left the school. Pictures are available of the participating students.

Most of the staff had first generation of relatives in foreign countries and they were interested in Hathaway's travels to most of the countries during LH's army assignment, she also had a letter of introduction from the University of Minnesota's School of Public Health to most of the countries' Public Health Departments in order to obtain material for a thesis. Hathaway continued night classes at the University of San Francisco. One of the Professors was fascinated and tried to develop an intimate relationship. The students observed the actions and began to tease Hathaway. She handled the situation. Today, a couple of those students remain as friends. One of the army nurses who has served with Hathaway, lived in the area and contributed to many happy events. She has since died but the family remains in contact.

Hathaway's mentor from her home made contact and asked that she accept one of the university students at Fisk who was expecting and after delivery, would return to her university. The student became a disaster. Hathaway could hardly wait for her to leave. The baby died; she became involved with unsavory type people. When one of the men involved with her decided he did not wish the friendship to continue, she attempted suicide.

The Hyatt area was becoming a dope den. This area was near where Hathaway was living with her classmate. One had to climb forty-two stairs to the apartment. LH was scheduled in six months to return stateside and he did not wish to live in or near the dope area. Nor did he want to climb the steps. He asked Hathaway to move into an apartment on the first floor level. She followed the request and moved into an apartment building on the first floor. Not for long did Hathaway remain in this environment because the owner would use a pass key and enter tenants' apartments whenever he wished.

One of the bridge players who was also a sorority sister rented one of her university student-type rooms to Hathaway. The relationship was excellent, more like relatives than landlordship. Today, the relationship continues. LH arrived and was pleased with the environment.

The Principal at the school invited LH and Hathaway to dinner before they left for assignment at Fort Lewis, Washington. The Principal shared the episode of the person who had impersonated Hathaway in order to get the assignment at his school. Relationship with this Principal continued until he died in 1994. Friendship between several of the teachers and a couple of students has continued throughout the years.

San Francisco had many historical features: the most crooked street in America, Fisherman's Wharf, Golden Gate Bridge, trolley cars. Across the San Francisco Bay Bridge into Oakland was only a stone's throw to Berkeley, where one may visit the University of California. The Route 101 scenic highway ran along the side of the Pacific Ocean, however, this highway could be very traumatic and dangerous. Night club life was out of sight. Hathaway enjoyed all types of music and the entertainment a place had to offer. Cannon Ball A and his brother lighted up the jazz sections for their music has never been forgotten. Cannon Ball's parents taught in the Florida University there Hathaway and LH had taught.

The student population at the schools was predominately Hispanic and Negroes. Whenever possible, Hathaway began to use Spanish with a few of the students. During the yearly school talent of choruses among all of the surrounding counties, Oakland Schools predominately all Negro students, each year for three years, ended up the most outstanding and received the trophy. All of the schools participating in the program had the students to wear attractive costumes predominately their school colors. The Oakland students wore black pants and skirts with white shirts or blouses, not in a uniform fashion, either the length of skirts, sleeves or blouses short or long. Hathaway had a conference with the students to suggest that they cooperate with uniformity and to congratulate them on having been endowed with such excellent talent.

At the end of the year, LH's assignment was Ft. Lewis, Washington.

WASHINGTON

The trip enroute to assignment at Fort Lewis was uneventful. Several army families welcomed LH and Hathaway and assisted them in getting settled. Once settled, Hathaway was hired by the city's Public Health Department which made her the first Negro nurse to be hired. There were very few Negroes in the area. Most of them were army families. This was an era of adjustment between the two races. Ironically, in 1945, Hathaway was with the Army Nurse Corps groups from the South Pacific which went by route of the Columbia River and landed in Tacoma, Washington. One of the Public Health nurses recalled having seen the nurses in the area. This was interesting, because she had not seen or heard of Negro nurses in the Army Nurse Corps. Reactions of the patients toward Hathaway on her first visit into their homes was not surprising because she had experienced the same reaction when she helped to develop services in an all white community in Michigan.

Several clients called the Director and stated that in the area was a Negro female driving a white station wagon and posing as a Public Health nurse. One should have heard their responses when asked what should they expect next. Whatever the Director told them must have been impressive because their attitudes and acceptance developed sooner than Hathaway had expected. Several staff members had to adjust to having a Negro co-worker. Rapport and friendship developed through weekend get-togethers in different members' homes. Few of the Negroes in the community resented a professional Negro and Hathaway changed their attitudes to acceptance.

Life began to settle into normal daily activities. Weekends filled in with bridge sessions, sorority meetings, dinner dances, tours to Vancouver Island, British Island, Mt. Rainier, exploring outlying cities, Olympia, the capital, Portland in Oregon for purchasing Pendelton clothing. The airport was between Tacoma and Seattle. Seattle, a well developed city, had most of a person's desires of various categories. Building of a highway road was in the process of permitting passage into Alaska. Many classmates and friends came to visit in order to take advantage of exploring the state of Washington. The greatest attraction in Seattle was the "Space Needle" towering over the city and suburbs. It contained several floors with a restaurant on the revolving top floor. Hathaway made sure that her guests were exposed to many attractions and highlighted their trip with a tour of Victoria, Canada. Guests on a Canadian ship would leave Seattle by way of the Pacific Ocean. After a three hour scenic atmosphere and Canandian food, they landed in Victoria, Canada. It was a very beautiful, quaint and interesting place with many English articles and fashions for sale.

The Board of Education had a staff of School Nurses, therefore the Public Health Nurses contact with children was limited to the handicaped and mentally retarded. Hathaway toured the Handicap facility in Yakima. This facility had patients from all over the United States; cases that Hathaway had never seen. One room had straps extended from the ceiling to hold the head of patients diagnosed with Hydrocephalus. The room accommodated hundreds of patients. There were extremely small male patients.

Neighbors on both sides of LH and Hathaway's army home became very friendly. One small boy of a neighbor developed a very close relationship and, whenever possible, he would go with Hathaway as if he were her son. When he entered school, he became very distant and told her that she was a Negro, therefore he did not want to go out with her. His mother became very upset because she had never discussed races. The family remained close friends for years after retirement from the army.

LH's brother and his family were assigned to Fort Lewis.

The brother had four daughters and one son. There was excellent rapport between the families. Hathaway practically took over the girls. Now that they are adults, they reminisce about those hilarious episodes.

Hathaway had been on the Public Health staff for a year when a co-worker told her that Pacific Lutheran University School of Nursing needed a teacher for the Maternal and Child Care Class. She applied for the position and was invited in for an interview. During the conference with the Dean, he hired her and advised her not to worry about being accepted by the faculty because she was the first Negro to be employed. Hathaway asked if she had been hired to teach the students or the faculty members because she could care less about their acceptance. There were only a few Negro students in the whole student body and only one Negro student nurse.

The School of Nursing Dean gave Hathaway the schedule and she was to schedule an appointment with the Chief Nurse at Madigan Army Hospital where the senior students were to practice. The chief nurse told Hathaway that the Department had decided to discontinue accepting the students because the methods and attitudes of the university instructor were not acceptable. However, the session with her sounded very promising and since she was an ex-Army nurse, she would accept the program again.

Hathaway's program in teaching always contained "C, I, A": Correlate, Integrate, and Associate, all principles of learning. This method was used in every program in which she had been involved and proved very rewarding. The students at Tuskegee change the failing status to very high state board examination scores.

Teaching at the university was most interesting. Madigan Army Hospital's maternal and child care unit was used for training and practical applications of principles. Many of the patients were foreign wives married to American soldiers. The students were enrolled in various foreign languages. When the wives went into labor, they would revert to their native languages. Hathaway assigned the students to patients who spoke the language in which the students were enrolled. Communication between the student and her patient was excellent. At the end of the nurse's training, the students wrote the State Board examination for license required to become a registered nurse. Hathaway's students made the highest score ever in the state of Washington. The American Nurses Association had Hathaway's biography published in Who's Who of American Women, 1967-68.

When President Kennedy visited the university, the staff formed a security line for him to the podium. As he walked through, he shook hands. He saw Hathaway, which was a surprise to him because he knew the university did not have Negroes on the faculty. He stepped back to her, hugged her and squeezed her hand. All of this action was on Tacoma's TV news report. For two days her home was filled with flowers, many congratulatory telegrams, letters, and phone calls from white and black people. Three months later, the President was assassinated. Several attempts have been made without results to recover the video tape of his walk through the line and the stop with Hathaway.

The President of the University never spoke to Hathaway because he did not want a Negro on his faculty. He would not have her listed or put in the school's Sage Book index for 1964. Her picture is in the book where she is teaching the students how to use the incubators, and she is listed in the Student Index of Saga '64. Should he see her approaching in the corridor, he would turn and go in the opposite direction. Her contract was not renewed at the end of the year, but after the American Nurses Association End of the Year Banquet announced that Hathaway's students had made a record of the highest score ever, the Dean of the School of Nursing wanted her to reconsider. The Tacoma Board of Education had made contact and asked Hathaway to join its staff as a school nurse with teaching credentials. She accepted the contract with the Board.

Tacoma's population was divided. Those in the metropolitan area were predominately Negro families whereas the area across the two bridges bordering Tacoma were all white families. Attitudes were the same as nation wide; some accepted and some did not. In order to accomplish her goals, Hathaway established a rapport with both races. The white families began to accept Hathaway, were very corrigible and cooperative in her school health programs. One teacher did not want her girls to see the film on menstruation but the parents overruled her. In one of the white schools, the school psychologist and Hathaway, in conjunction with Stanford University, developed a dyslexia program. By the same token, she and the student counselor in the predominately Negro Junior High had to help with students who had serious personal hygiene problems. The counselor obtained Hathaway's aid in actually bathing the students in the counselor's home. She was white and really interested in helping the students.

When Hathaway had to have minor surgery and LH had been sent to Europe, this counselor brought hot meals daily to Hathaway before she herself had eaten. Today, contact remains.

One day as Hathaway made rounds in the predominately black second grade (Black students with a white teacher), she noticed the students had been dismissed, but the teacher was in tears. Upon investigation, the teacher had given the students Christmas gifts. Several had returned the gifts and stated that their mother told them that she was white and did not like them, therefore to give back the gifts. The teacher and Hathaway were U. of Minnesota graduates. Since she was a single person, Hathaway told her to hell with the students' parents and for her to apply for a teaching position in the army schools in Europe. Pressure had to be applied several weeks before she followed up on the suggestion. An assignment was immediately available in an Army elementary school near Stuttgart. She and a co-worker visited Hathaway and LH quite often in Heidelburg. She married an Army Major while they were in Germany, had two children, and is now retired on the west coast. Today contact remains. When they were stationed in Ohio, and LH and Hathaway visited, the young baby was shy to go to Hathaway. His mother said, "Go to Hathaway; she is responsible for you being here!" The father said, "Really?" We all laughed!

Hathaway developed a teenage student program with her Tacoma AKA sorority. The program contained all phases of teenagers' developmental stages in life with intentions of pursuing his or her potential in order to be an asset in one's life and society. She had the same type of program in the school for any student interested. One white student's parents were so appreciative of Hathaway helping their daughter through high school, then into nurses training, they brought all kinds of vegetables from their farm to her throughout the summer. She would come home from work to find vegetables at her door.

Hathaway and LH developed a scholarship fund in the name of her mentor, Gwendolyn Chandler, who had financially helped her through most of her life when she taught Hathaway in elementary, then high school. The fund was to assist indigent students with desires to pursue college degrees. Contact was made with organizations to contribute or develop scholarship funds. Several organizations would give donations. One Negro male student who was selected from the German class as an exchange student in Germany did not have funds and was prepared to give up. Several organizations, including the NAACP, gave Hathaway donations to assist her in sending the student to Germany. After such care, the student returned, graduated from school and later became an outlaw, a ruthless person.

Christmas, when Hathaway visited in Germany, the Board of Education had her to visit the exchange students. She had to reprimand the male student during the visit. The white female student was well loved and accepted by the German family. The German family who had accepted the male student was very happy when his exchange visit ended.

Another distasteful episode involved one of Hathaway's Negro female students. The student was interested in attending the Seattle College and her mother and relatives tried to discourage enrollment but encouraged her to find a maid's job like they had. Hathaway obtained half of the sorority's scholarship fund, had the student to enroll, picked her up and demanded her mother accompany them to the college so that the mother would know where her daughter was living. The student was very intelligent and was given a scholarship from the college to obtain a Master's degree. She became one of the teachers in Tacoma.

Hathaway enrolled in night classes at Pacific Lutheran University to continue work toward her Master's Degree in Education, majoring in math. One of her instructors became very interested and would tutor her in math. Many of the faculty members remembered when she taught at the University and were disappointed when she left the staff.

This was the year when Junior Colleges were developing. The Tacoma Board of Education sent Hathaway to San Francisco as a delegate to obtain materials and information to establish the two-year nursing program in the developing Junior College in Tacoma. Deans from all over the United States attended the conference. Hathaway's past Dean from the University of Minnesota School of Public Health was happy to see Hathaway there and asked her to reconsider returning to the University of Minnesota for her Master's Degree, that she had heard and read so many outstanding things she had accomplished since graduating from the U. of Minnesota and was sorry that in the beginning, she was not accepted into the graduate program. Other delegates overheard the conversation and laughed. Hathaway was the first Black to graduate from U. of Minn. School of Public Health Nursing in 1952 on the G.I. Bill.

LH was stationed in Heidelberg, Germany, and had begun to ask Hathaway to resign from her job and join him. The personnel officer was quite disappointed when Hathaway submitted her resignation. He told her that a position on the School Nurse program would always be available. Hathaway was rather reluctant to leave. She wanted to stay in Tacoma to review the progress of the different programs she had developed involving the students, especially the Dyslexia program. The schools and friends had many farewell parties. The ex co-worker teachers in San Francisco heard that she was leaving for Germany, therefore they made contact that they planned to visit and they gave addresses of first generation relatives in Europe for her visit.

The trip by ship was uneventful as compared to the first trip over in 1954. Segregation was not apparent. LH met the tour bus with roses. Hathaway shared the roses with another army wife and then proceeded to the army quarters. Their little poodle dog had arrived a week before and was accepted by an airport sales frau who had been a friend for years when they were stationed in Hanau in 1954. In fact, their first Schnauzer dog was purchased from her family and this dog was used to get Hathaway to accept pets.

Once again their home was in an army compound. Activities

began. Hathaway became enrolled in the University of Maryland, German class only. She wanted it on her transcript because prior to this she had studied German from a private tutor in Aberdeen, Maryland, before the first trip to Hanau, Germany. Once in Hanau, she had a private tutor, now this would be recorded. Through the years she had continued to communicate in German with her foster German families.

In Heidelberg, the American School had a vacancy in the school health program. Since Hathaway was in in Hanau 1955, when the American Red Cross had developed this program, she applied. The Principal refused to hire her, stated a white officer's wife had preference. The American Nurses Association became quite angry because she had developed this program and, since her arrival, she had participated in the school immunization and health classes.

The American Nurses Association elected Hathaway as President. In conjunction with the army hospital, the Association took care of the outpatient clinics. Hathaway had many activities, one of outpatient maternal and child health classes. Expectant fathers would view the movie on childbirth. Occasionally one or two would faint. Planned tours were made of various German health facilities that had developed after the war. The expertise from American doctors had helped the Germans to evaluate their health needs. Prior to VE day, the Germans never felt that children needed mental health care. Therefore American operated facilities were developed.

During the holidays and summer sessions the American Board of Education had tours into other countries. Hathaway took advantage of the opportunity because she had lists of former coworkers' relatives she was to visit. A Mission High School teacher in San Francisco had relatives in Israel. Hathaway took them coffee, checked the Wailing Wall and said a prayer. The beatitude area was beautiful. She explored Bethelehem, Jerusalem, and Jordan, where Nomadic people were living, took a wade in the Dead Sea, checked the recently opened Center for Children "Kibbutz Centers." The hotel was well kept and from the window, one could have an excellent overview of Israel. Hathaway checked Jesus' birth and burial places. Next, came

Egypt. The hotel in Cario was filled with roaches; one had to keep suitcases closed. The streets were crowded with men in pajama type suits, begging for money. To the pyramids, Hathaway rode on a horse and buggy drawn cart. She then mounted a camel just for a picture of the visiting group. When the group was ready to leave Cario, at the bus station, soldiers cornered Hathaway and began to interrogate her about Martin Luther King's assassination. She told them that she was living in Germany during the episode. They ignored her and began to make her walk to their headquarters. The Supervisor of the trip had a difficult time getting Hathaway free. Next stop was a tour of the museums with tombs, statues, etc. People lived in the cemetery with their buried relatives. Before the visit, the government had ordered the people to move out and orders were ignored. Hitchcock made a movie of the situation. On a visit to one of the mosques, each had to remove his or her shoes. Marble walls contained a design of the Masonic Lodge.

Athens, Greece, was the first city to build an athletic field and during the visit, a tour was made of where, once upon a time, chariots graced the field. A Greek relative of Hathaway's co-worker in San Francisco came to visit during her stay in Greece. Pictures were taken of Hathaway walking down from the Temple of Acropolis (fortified hill) the Citadel of Athens.

Beirut was a beautiful city. A female and male teacher of Boston University and Hathaway were housed in a most beautiful French hotel. One of Hathaway's co-workers at Pacific Lutheran University in Tacoma had a home and family in Beirut. Her brother was a doctor there. The three made a tour of the oldest city in the world.

The group took the plane from the airport near the Mediterranean Sea and it seemed as if the plane was going to land in the sea but it made it up and returned to end the trip in Frankfurt. Hathaway has many pictures and slides of the month long trip.

Hathaway's home was like Grand Central Station, integrated with ex co-workers, San Francisco and Tacoma Washington nursing classmate, exchange students from the Tacoma School., Army buddies of prior assignments; never a dull moment. One white, ex co-worker had married and had a baby boy and when they came to visit, they would leave the baby and take short trips to visit relatives in Israel; the same relatives Hathaway had visited in Israel. The white Assistant Principal in Tacoma brought his wife and stayed with Hathaway. Beds were all over the house, from the maid's quarters in the basement to a folding cot for Hathaway's classmate in LH and Hathaway's bedroom.

Across the hall, the family would visit and ask Hathaway to babysit their baby boy. He has become a nurse. The mother, an Australian, died some time ago in Denver. The son and father keep in touch. Upstairs, the family's son in high school relied on Hathaway to check his homework and art projects. He showed tendencies of becoming an outstanding artist. He did a painting as a gift, beautiful, it stays on display. He wrote when he enrolled in art at a university in Denver, Colorado.

Next door army wive's sisters from Illinois came to visit. Hathaway drove them on sight seeing trips in surrounding areas of Heidelberg. When the sisters returned to Illinois, they gave Hathaway a beautiful set of crystal glasses with gold bands. She has five of the six to this day. They submitted her accomplishments in life to their group and, in turn, sent Hathaway a sterling silver tray engraved: "Golden Year Award - Southern District I.A.C.W. 1968". Occasional contact is continued today.

A daughter of a family from Hathaway's home town was an army wife. She and her husband had adopted a baby. She would come to visit for lessons on baby care. When they left Heidelberg and settled in a city not too far from where Hathaway lived, there was no more contact whatever.

A white Army dentist enrolled in the University of Maryland German class with Hathaway. They began to study together and he would bring his baby girl in her basket bed and place it the center of Hathaway's bed. The baby is now a young lady and has a Master's Degree in German and Spanish. Contact continued through the years. Her father is a dentist in the suburb of Chicago and is a Lionel train nut!! He and his wife attend all of the train conferences wherever every year.

An African doctor and nurse wife became very friendly which boiled down to their friendship was only to use Hathaway by asking her to purchase items from the comissary or PX. She immediately ended the contact.

LH was interested in art, therefore he took many trips to Florence, Italy's art museums. When Hathaway's classmate came, he and Hathaway planned a trip to the various countries. She was Catholic, therefore Italy was first on the itinerary; into Rome, a tour of the Vatican, with Michelangelo art in most of the rooms, the tourists were housed in a Catholic facility with meals that were most tasteful. Venice known for beautiful artistic glass manufacturers, with displays throughout the city and both sides of the canal, and where LH, her classmate and Hathaway rode on the gondola. She was really frightened because there were three fat people and the driver of the gondola just laughed at her remark about their sizes. Gondolas are long, narrow flat bottomed boats used on the canal. There were families living on the opposite sides of the canal. The next tour was the home of Florence Nightingale who developed the first nurses' training program and, down the street, was supposed to be the birthplace of Sarah Gamp, a most outrageous dirty nurse.

Two weeks, and the tour continued into the Isle of Capri. Hathaway bought a beautiful dress and hat in one of the shops on this island. Next stop was Piza and the leaning tower; Milan and a tour of the famous Opera House. Naples was an ordinary, dirty city with skyline and clothesline for the apartment building tenants. The bus tour continued into Switzerland, with shopping in Zurich and the return to Heidelberg.

Once the house was clear of visitors and back to normal, Hathaway settled into her routine daily living. This period was short-lived. LH had been exposed to all types of music. His mother majored in piano and he, in school, played a cello. He invited a group of army musicians and one, who was white, was married to a black girl. She was in training for opera voice. There were many sessions with army families, and Germans and Americans visiting relatives. One of the black musicians, after his discharge, settled in Rochester, N.Y. and teaches in the public school system. Hathaway was a dear friend of Count Basie, Duke Ellington and their band members. She would take many friends to their concerts in Germany. Hathaway was a dancer and from high school had danced when Jimmy Lunceford, Eddie Randall and Seven Blue Devils, and guitarist L. Mith from St. Louis all played at her school affairs. They continued friendship through the years.

Hathaway began the second semester German class and during the session, fell unconscious and was admitted into the army hospital and was diagnosed with hypertension. The condition continues to the present time. After being placed on medication, Hathaway continued wherever voluntary service was needed.

The German instructor had become friendly with Hathaway. The first semester she had received a grade of "A." When she became ill, the instructor learned that Hathaway was an ex army nurse and had a degree from the University of Minnesota. She thought that Hathaway was studying for a degree. Next semester, she was given a "C" and the instructor ended the friendship.

FORT HUACHUCA, ARIZONA

LH received orders for Fort Huachuca, Arizona, a return to the fort where it began for him and Hathaway in World War II with assignment to the South Pacific. Outside of the fort's gate during World War II, was an undeveloped "Frygate" area with dirty one-room houses used for Mexican prostitutes; no running water, venereal diseases at a high rate among the soldiers. Thank goodness all of past history had been replaced with lucrative well-developed areas; Hucachuca City and Serra Vista had more to offer. Tucson was no longer a bland mud pack city. Many army families had settled in this area. School buses ran all over outlying areas.

Hathaway began voluntary assignments with the Red Cross, blood bank office, immunization program, maternal and child health classes and first aid classes. The Catholic school in Bisbee asked her to temporarily fill a vacancy. Daily rides over the mountain became too stressful, therefore at the end of the school year she refused to renew the contract. The students were very upset because they had become attached to her. They expressed their feelings in poems and small gifts. The nuns did not want to accept her resignation. During the summer, they would go to an area in Michigan for retreat. Many years later Hathaway met the aunt of one of her students from Bisbee School. He is now a psychologist.

One day as Hathaway left the commissary, four male high

school students asked for a ride home. Three white students lived in her area and the black students' family lived in Serra Vista. They made up a musical combo and asked if she would help them to make a musical tape in the army recording office. LH contacted their director and they proceeded to record on tape. This was the era of dope entering the United States and this city was at the border of Mexico. Students had begun to use dope. When the tape was finished, Hathaway had it played on the radio. The point was to encourage the students to think twice before becoming involved in dope and to hear how well some classmates were making it.

Hathaway had the newspaper run an article about the Junior High musical students. The radio news report commented and played the tape. Various business owners donated funds when Hathaway made contact to help the students' musical project. The Superintendent of the Board of Education heard about her voluntary Red Cross work and the students musical program and asked her to become a substitute teacher in both elementary and secondary schools. She accepted his offer because the director of the combo was an Army soldier and when he was sent out to another camp, his relief director was surprised to see a Negro female practically running the program. He became very insulting, therefore Hathaway left the group and became a substitute teacher.

The first assignment was with fifth graders. Classes were held in a rented room in one of the closed army hospitals where Hathaway had once been an army nurse. The students were bussed in. Once the school was finished in Serra Vista, the army room was closed. The students became attached to Hathaway and would practically knock her down to introduce her to their parents when out shopping. There was only one other black teacher in the area and she was assigned in the Junior High chemistry department (the other black high school teacher was on sabbatical leave to become a student at Arizona University.) LH was in a graduate class and had not obtained his Bachelors degree. One of the students questioned this and was informed that LH was the only A grade student in the class, so mind his business. Hathaway enrolled in Political Science class.

Again Hathaway's house was like Grand Central Station. Many friends came to visit. One of the Negro student's mother came from her home. They became friends and Hathaway encouraged her to enroll at the University. She now has an outstanding position in a government agency in Florida. Another white student became a dope user and committed suicide. Her fifth grade sister became hysterical and accepted only her ex-teacher Hathaway. She had to spend two days and nights to calm her. Her parents never forgot Hathaway.

A high school teacher asked Hathaway if she would become a mentor for one of the Negro female (very intelligent) students, that the student doesn't have money to enter into the recently developed Chochise College. Hathaway accepted the responsibility and what a "crock." LH and she paid the fee for cap and gown, prom clothing and college entrance fee. The Army father received orders and the mother decided to live in Tucson. The student really did not wish to further her education, therefore the mother attempted to withdraw the college entrance fee. Hathaway had moved to Michigan when the college contacted her and sent her the refund.

It was discovered the LH was diabetic and, upon discharge, he was offered a civilian job on the army post. He refused because he had planned to return to Michigan, the Superintendent of the Cochise County Schools offered a permanant job to Hathaway, one of her choice, elementary or secondary. The four combo band students she had introduced to the public, had a farewell dinner and presented a beautiful gold pin to always remember them and show how much they appreciated her help. Hathaway really did not wish to leave Arizona. She had visited friends in Phoenix where one had an opportunity to shop in the outstanding "Mall" with a camel back shaped mountain. Arizona was becoming a prosperous state. After many farewell parties, she and LH hit the road.

1969 MICHIGAN

An uneventful cross country drive with two automobiles. They decided to settle in Detroit. LH's aunt lived alone in a large house on the west side. LH went to work at the Veterans office on Baltimore Street. Hathaway began as night charge nurse in a TB ward at the Veterans Hospital in Allen Park. Once again she encountered problems. The two white night supervisors resented her background of having a degree. They asked her why she did not apply for the afternoon Supervisor position since she was degree qualified. Hathaway told them she did not wish an afternoon job. Whenever there was an opportunity, they tried to irritate her. Finally Hathaway sent in her resignation. The Director of the hospital had appointed her to represent the hospital at the "Equal Employment Opportunity Council" that was meeting in Ohio. He asked her to please reconsider. The chief nurse had the personnel officer come to her office. While Hathaway was present, the two asked her to reconsider; that they wanted her to conduct classes on "Principles of Supervision" for the staff. Hathaway told them that it would be a waste of time to try to change the old "Biddies" attitudes and she would rather not. The two night supervisors were very happy because she intimidated them but they had a lovely farewell luncheon when she left. The night staff was very disappointed.

LH and Hathaway found a recently developed housing area to move in from his aunt's house. The Lafayette Clinic was in the area. Hathaway thought it was a clinic but when she went in for a job she learned that it was an institution for the mentally and psychiatric ill patients. The chief nurse persuaded her to accept the night supervisory position. She accepted but Public Health was her "bag," not institutions. Since she had majored in math at Pacific Lutheran University in Tacoma, by day, she became a substitute teacher with the Detroit Public School System.

The chief nurse was black and had a reputation of being very mean to black personnel. She knew that Hathaway wanted a position involving Public Health. When a clinic was developed within the hospital, she assigned one of the white nurses who did not have training or a degree. Only the chief nurse and three black nurses had a degree in the entire hospital staff. When the assistant director, who was white, left, only three black nurses remained with degrees.

Again, as had happened in Heidelberg where Hathaway first fainted in class, she fainted in her kitchen. A neighbor doctor came immediately and diagnosed a problem with hypertension. She knew why the flare-up!! Too much activity by night; nurse supervisor and by day, math teacher. The next night when she reported for duty, two of the staff nurses fussed and began to fight on duty. Hathaway read the policies to the two and sent them home. That morning, the director told her that she should have followed another method. Hathaway had planned to resign, now stated that "God takes care of babies and fools." This episode gave her a good reason to resign and take away the stress. She became a full time substitute with the Detroit Board of Education.

Her substitute teacher assignment began in an east side elementary trouble shooters and disturbed teenagers in special section of the school. The beginning of Hathaway's assignment was confined to the elementary students. From the kindergarten up, she taught history, maps, children slides in the various countries, exports and imports of these countries, aided the students with art drawings from their observation of their surroundings. In all of her classes she had students participate in the Michigan Week celebration and entered their drawings of the map of Michigan with the robin as the state bird. The prizes were to be given as first, second, third. Hathaway contacted a company that had packages of six types of cereals and, when she explained that all of the students would be given a prize to encourage and show their appreciation of trying to accomplish something in life, the company gave free, all the packages she needed. The students asked why all of them received a gift. She explained that all of her students had tried.

Different food imports were discussed and when Hathaway had samples of Edam cheese shown on the slides, the students were eager to try the cheese. One mother came to meet Hathaway and stated her kindergarten daughter had her purchase the cheese at the Eastern Market and her family loved the taste. They learned that cocoa from Africa, was sent into Hershey, Pennsylvania, the capital of chocolate.

The school was predominately black students. One white student in the fifth grade was treated badly; the students would take his lunch money, beat on him, and call him names. The one student responsible had been reprimanded over and over with no results. When Hathaway walked into the room, the black student called him "Honkey." She made the white student say, "Shut up Nigger." The black student bristled with fist folded. Hathaway asked him if he found out how it feels to be called names. He apologized and thereafter the two treated each other as human beings and became close friends.

The instructor, Mrs. Taylor, for the disturbed students, fell and fractured her leg. The principal assigned Hathaway to the class. The teenage girls had many problems; were not interested in an education; promiscuity was their greatest interest. They had to be made to prepare their lunch food, would not use precaution with the washing machines, were fairly cooperative when shampooed and pressed their hair, would practice make-up with cosmetic equipment, not be too cooperative with the academic material and occasionally would refuse to use the showers. Hathaway and a co-worker took the group on a tour of Battle Creek-Kellogg and thereafter to dinner. She had to teach them how to write and address the free post cards given to tourists. Except for one, they ate properly at the dinner party in the hotel.

Two of the students were sent from juvenile court to a facility for girls in Adrian, Michigan. One of the girls refused to go because she did not have the clothing that one must have. Hathaway bought all the clothing, took it to her home and gave it to her mother. She never received the clothing and continued to refuse, to go, therefore she ended up in the Wayne County Youth Home. All traces were erased and never again was contact made with her.

Ms. Taylor, the instructor Hathaway had relieved, became very angry about Hathaway's excellent progress with many of the girls and therefore tried to make trouble for Hathaway. The assistant Principal received an assignment of Principal in another school and asked Hathaway to accompany her to the new school. The Principal wrote an excellent resume and recommendation for Hathaway and asked her to remain at his school, in the same position and he would assign Mrs. Taylor, the teacher she had relieved, to another section. Hathaway refused to cause trouble and went with the Principal to her new elementary school assignment on the west side. Hathaway became remedial math and relief teacher in the school. The elementary school sent its students to the Junior High in the backyard of its school.

The kindergarten students' instructor became ill for about a month and Hathaway substituted. She taught the students to answer roll call in foreign languages of their choice: German, French or Spanish! All except one used the system; he stated he did not want to and would continue with only English, "Good morning." His classmates reprimanded him and Hathaway informed the students that it was his privilege to choose. This student is now a doctor in Atlanta, Georgia. When the teacher returned, Hathaway was assigned as remedial math instructor. The regular instructor had taken a sabbatical six week leave. The students missed her and they were rather reluctant to accept a substitute. Once they got to know Hathaway, everything turned out well.

The students in the school where Hathaway had relieved Ms. Taylor continued to make contact. Ms. Taylor apologized about her actions and began to visit or invite Hathaway to her home for family affairs; even borrowed money from her when necessary. When Hathaway visited Australia, she visited Ms. Taylor's daughter who was an exchange teacher there.

The math teacher returned and Hathaway became the relief for a short period. One of the teachers became assistant principal in another district and offered Hathaway a position to develop a remedial math program in her school. Hathaway accompanied her to the school on the far east side. The neighborhood was predominately white with black families beginning to move in to integrate the area. Most of the white adults who could not financially move out were afraid. Several of the adults taught their children to cause problems in the school.

During Halloween, with a mask on, a white fifth grade student, who left the school and enrolled in a private school, met her black friend after school. She told the black student to tell her mother that Hathaway had slapped her face and pulled her hair. There was a white student with the same name as the black student. She was in Hathaway's math remedial class and the black student was not. When the principal had the black student and Hathaway meet in his office, Hathaway was shocked to see her instead of the white student who was in the remedial class. The student had been progressing exceptionally well and was to be released back into the regular math class. When Hathaway asked the black student when, where and why she had been slapped, she began to cry and stated that her kindergarten sister had told her to say that. When questioned further, she stated her white girlfriend had met her after school and told her to tell her mother that Hathaway had done that to her. When asked who was the friend and her name, the student began to cry again and said, "I don't know her name because she had on a mask." Hathaway was standing back of the lying student, stepped back and began to laugh. The principal had to keep a straight face. He turned very red, called the student's mother immediately and she apologized for her daughter.

Mrs. Johns, a white secretary of the Parent Teachers Association would not allow her first grade daughter to remain in the classroom when Hathaway gave basis math principles. The daughter had to go and sit in the principal's office until the class ended. Her fifth grade daughter had to attend the math classes and would try to create problems.

The president of the PTA became a school board council member and left the school. Hathaway had told her students that she was going to Germany for the summer and might return as relief teacher, not math. Many of the students wrote or made cards with messages that they loved her. Even Mrs. Johns' first grade daughter printed a note that ended with, "I love you." Hathaway kept her note for years. At the end of the year, Hathaway had ordered the update equipment borrowed from the school she had left to come to this school. When she returned from Germany and reported to the school, the equipment she had for a replacement teacher, was not in the room. The principal told Hathaway that she would have to again teach remedial math because no one wanted the assignment. Hathaway asked where was the equipment she had ordered. The remedial reading teacher had become coordinator of the Remedial Reading and Remedial Math programs and the principal had her to come to the office and inquired where was the equipment Hathaway had ordered. Her reply was that the budget had been cut, therefore Hathaway's request had to be eliminated. Hathaway said. "Like hell! If I am to teach remedial math, I need the update equipment too. I am returning the borrowed equipment I brought in here from the other school!" Within a couple of hours, the delivery man came in with Hathaway's order and stated that he questioned the remedial reading and not the remedial math request that was delivered a week before. The Remedial Reading Coordinator came into Hathaway's office and took care of her assignments. After the feuds, the relationship became professional and tolerant.

In the teacher's lounge, the teachers began to criticize one of the junior high student, an adolescent about how his odor filled the room, therefore windows had to be opened. Hathaway asked the teachers if they were aware that one should think of physical and mental health changes in a teenager. After school, she asked the student be sent to to my room. When the student arrived, the younger students wanted to know why he was in their room. They were told that he had come to move some boxes. They wanted to move the boxes and finally accepted the explanation and left for home. A conference with the student covered body changes in adolescence, washing machine, toothpaste, clothing, food for breakfast and dinner. Hathaway informed him to wash his clothing so that clean clothing would be available every day following his shower; if no toothpaste was available, then use baking soda with or without salt and baking soda under the axillary area. Since "Afro" hair was the style, Hathaway picked his hair and instructed him to pick it daily. The students in her classes with "Afro" hair styles had the hair picked daily. After the conference, the student followed up on all advice given and each day stopped by Hathaway's room so that she could inspect him and see how neat he looked. Those picks are in storage.

Remedial math classes gave Hathaway an opportunity to include principles of health, different languages, encourage them to treat each other individually rather than think and treat people collectively. They were shown slides of children throughout the world with more information about the ones Hathaway had had personal contact work in many countries and continues today with those in Australia and Germany.

Hathaway had the "Les Cochon Bleau" (Blue Pigs) policemen visit the school. The students were excited and very appreciative in seeing and hearing policemen perform. They gave the students inspiration and encouragement to continue in school, obtain an education and make something good of their lives. After such contact, fear of policemen decreased.

Most of the students in the math class did fairly well and were ready to return to the normal class. They were grateful and wrote many notes of thanks and how much they loved Hathaway. She had a small store made by one of her co-workers at Lafayette Clinic. He is an artist and developed the store box with slots for insertions of various articles for sale. Hathaway gave each student different amounts of money to shop at the store. They were given enough, not enough for two to three articles, and a layaway plan. They because very excited over such an activity in math.

One of her former teacher-aid ladies was an artist and made picturesque alphabet that Hathaway strung on a clothesline. She had the students spell words by singing or walking under the letters used.

When Hathaway gave up teaching, she gave most of her equipment to one of her teacher friends. Occasionally Hathaway would use a stethoscope and have her students check each others' pulse and listen to the heartbeat. The students were elated and told their parents. They even checked their families' pulses. Several of the parents called and thanked Hathaway for teaching their children.

The principal gave Hathaway her evaluation report and she noticed that "Parent Relationship" did not receive outstanding as on the previous evaluation. She recalled a run in with the remedial reading teacher who had become coordinator of the two remedial math and reading. Too, the mother, president of the Parent Teachers Conference, did not want black teachers to teach her children and she had her daughter go to the Principal's office during her schedule in the remedial math sessions. However, she had no control when Hathaway relieved the kindergarten teacher. Her daughter in the class refused to leave and sent a very sincere note of how much she loved Hathaway when she heard of her leaving the school.

The assistant principal's daughter had a wedding reception and, at the reception, the principal asked Hathaway if she would reconsider and return to his school. Hathaway's husband told him no way...she was not returning to his school. The principal's wife stated, "Why don't you say the same about me?"

Hathaway gave up working and began volunteering in the schools for her sorority's remedial reading program. She and two of the army nurses decided to return to visit friends in Australia and New Guinea area. It was most exciting and pleasant to revisit families, with tours to the Koalas and kangaroo farms, Island of Birds and the "Oyster Shell" opera house in Sydney. The opera house is one of the best known and great buildings of the world. There were pictures of America's outstanding people: Count Basie, Duke Ellington, Ella Fitzgerald, etc.

The visit gave an opportunity to meet Ms. Taylor's daughter and other U.S. teachers assigned to Australia. It was on this visit that the Australian Press was at the airport and wanted to take pictures of a celebrity, Mrs. Henry Kissinger. They interviewed Hathaway so that when she spoke to Mrs. Kissinger they could take her picture. Mrs. Kissinger broke her security line to come over to Hathaway, shook her hand and the two had an interesting conversation. This episode appeared in the Brisbane newspapers. The comrades had a farewell dinner party with all of their Austrialian friends. Before returning to the United States, Hathaway sent postcards to her remedial class children, They were elated to hear from her.

Upon returning from the visit in Australia, Hathaway increased her area of volunteer program of immunization for children, flu shots for the elderly and remedial math volunteering in the schools. When she was not involved, time was spent with her lounging on the couch viewing TV programs. Once during one of these sessions, a public health nurse friend came to visit and was shocked to see Hathaway idle on a couch. She told her to return to work. This friend was employed by the State of the Minority Employment Agency. She told Hathaway that she would not encourage employment there because Hathaway did not have the patience nor compassion for blacks who did not prepare themselves according to capabilities. When Hathaway sent an application to the State Public Health Department, a retired Army nurse-chief nurse of the State Mental Health Department checked the roster seeking a nurse for the department. She saw Hathaway's application and on it was that she was an army nurse. The chief nurse took her application out of the Public Health section and immediately called Hathaway to offer her a position in her department: "Mental Health." LH and Hathaway went to the State Department, 95 miles, for a conference with the Director. The session lasted only ten minutes to tell her to report for duty at the local office, only ten miles from her home.

This job was a new adventure for Hathaway. It required driving over the state of Michigan; areas that were not too well developed, some areas not accustomed to a Negro in their outlying homeland. Indians inhabited isolated areas in the upper peninsula. Now, a lot of those areas have Casinos. Many a person had no idea that Mental Health and Psychiatric facilities existed in these outlying areas. When the State Department staff visited these facilities, the staff was most cooperative naturally, because they wanted accreditation to continue.

This new adventure had many challengers. Several staff members resented Hathaway's assigned supervision on various tours. The only other black was a male person hired six months before she joined the staff, therefore he resented her assignment as supervisor. On one assignment, he attempted trouble that received a negative reaction from the Director.

The Department offices for staff members were frequently changed and that required lengthy drives. Most of the facilities for evaluation were far apart, therefore that gave one the knowledge of the extreme differences in the state's territory. One area was borderlined by another state's village that was inhabited by Mormons. A visit of the village was exciting, to see their typical horse and buggy transportation. In the restaurants, the food was delicious: served family style as served in Frankenmuth. Many visits were made in underdeveloped, wilderness areas that were primitive: dirt roads inhabited mostly with Indians and a few prejudiced whites who resented Hathaway evaluating their techniques, patient care and written records.

Later, state cars were discontinued and mileage paid for use of personal cars. Mileage pay was insufficient for the wear and tear on the car. However, good events counteracted dissatisfaction. Hathaway was sent as delegate to the National Convention of Mental Health meeting held in Denver, Colorado. This gave her an opportunity to visit with alumni members whom she had never known.

The Director, who had hired Hathaway, transferred to the National Mental Health Department. This department evaluated four states' programs and progress. Her replacement was a young male who had various assignments with the state, and after amalgamation and closing of various departments, he became the Director.

The same three staff members who resented Hathaway occasionally as Supervisor on survey trips, attempted to encourage him to change her status. He completely ignored their ridicule and told them that her attributes were outstanding.

On one of the survey trips, a patient attempted to escape and ran into Hathaway standing in his path. She received a severe injury to her left wrist when she raised her arm to block his blow. She had to have surgery.

Upon recovery and having to drive ninety-five miles to her office. Hathaway, after four years, began to evaluate and think of retirement. The new Director told her that he appreciated her attributes and did not want her to retire. Today, contact continues with a couple of the co-workers, secretaries, the Director and facilities' staff members.

Hathaway began to do voluntary work with several organizations. She nursed the sister of her secretary friend she had met at the VA in Michigan. The sister had cancer and died. The family through the years have continued contact. The mother of these girls lived to be a hundred years old.

RETIREMENT

Upon retirement, Hathaway decided to develop a project of pictures of the African American Army nurses to inform the world of their contributions during World War II. The Army Nurse Corps was established in 1901. The Women's Auxiliary Army Corps was developed and later changed to the Women's Army Corps (WAC). Many people think that all black women were WACs; they do not know that black nurses were inducted as officers into the Army Nurse Corps, whereas women of the WAC were officers according to their educational backgrounds.

In 1941, prior to the attack on Pearl Harbor, the Armed Forces of the United States reactivated the Army Nurse Corps and began to increase the Nurse Corps by recruiting nurses. Since the Armed Forces were segregated, the Army Nurse Corps was not accepting Afro American Nurses.

Due to intervention by Mrs. Eleanor Roosevelt, Mrs. Mary McLoud Bethune, Educator, and Mrs. Mable Staupers, R.N., President of the now defunct Negro Graduate Nurses Association, the Surgeon General stipulated to them that a quota of only forty-eight African American nurses would be accepted as commissioned officers into the Army Nurse Corps.

Twenty-four nurses were sent to Fort Bragg, North Carolina,

and twenty-four were sent to Camp Livingston, Louisiana. Shortly thereafter, Camp Livingston was closed and the twenty-four nurses were dispersed to Fort Bragg, N.C., and For Huachuca, Arizona. The attack on Pearl Harbor eliminated the quota, increasing the number of nurses accepted. Contingents from the two stations were deployed to various areas within the continental United States and Overseas.

Fort Bragg now had its full complement of nurses. This group of 24 had come to Fort Bragg from many sections of the Country and represented many Nursing Schools. They are as follows: Lincoln School for Nurses, New York City; Emmie Perkins, Louise Jacobs, Ruth Briggs, Kathryn Bough; Gady Hospital, Atlanta Georgia: Lillie Emory, Gladys Giles,; Piedmont Hospital, Burkeville, Virginia: Inez Holmes; Provident Hospital, Chicago, Illinois: Esther Stewart, Susanne Davis; Spellman College Hospital, Atlanta, Georgia: Mria August; University Hospital, Augusta, Georgia; Margarette Kendrick; Brewster Hospital, Jacksonville, Florida: Margaret Ivory; Mercy Hospital, Philadelphia, Pennsylvania: Rose Elliott, Gertrude Scott; Freedman's Hospital, Washington, D. C.: Mary Petty; Community Hospital, Wilmington, North Carolina: Daisy Evans: Provident Hospital, Baltimore, Maryland: Lena Jones, Bessie A. Richardson; St. Agnes Hospital, Raleigh, North Carolina: Ruth Speight; Minnesota General Hospital, Minneapolis, Minnesota: Theresa James; John Andrew Memorial Hospital, Tuskegee, Alabama: Pharfoena Jones.

At Camp Livingston, Louisiana, 24 Negro nurses were serving in that Station Hospital. They, too, come from many sections of the country and represented many Nursing Schools. They are as follows: Freedmen's Hospital, Washington, D.C.: Susan E. Freeman, M. Crezet Ward; University Hospital, Augusta, Georgia: Elsie Helen Wallace, Josie Glenn; Lincoln School for Nurses, New York City: Helen L. Fisher; Hubbard Hospital, Meharry Medical School, Nashville, Tennessee: Willie Mae Bailey; John A. Andrew Memorial Hospital, Tuskegee Institute, Alabama: Ida Mae Burley; Provident Hospital, Baltimore, Maryland: Susan F. Harris, Margaret Ann Key, Mary Sarah Holmes; St. Phillips Hospital, Medical College of Virginia, Richmond, Virginia: Norma L. Greene, Josephine A. Cherry: Mercy

Hospital School for Nurses, Philadelphia, Pennsylvania: Daryle E. Foister; Homer G. Phillips Hospital, St. Louis, Missouri: Mary Jane Hester; Hampton Institute, Hampton, Virginia: Beatrice Elizabeth Hill; Macon Hospital Training School, Macon, Georgia: Mattie L. Thomas Aikens; Kansas City General Hospital #2, Kansas City, Missouri; Ora D. Pierce, Esther L. Allen, Abbie Voorhees; St. Agnes Hospital, Raliegh, North Carolina: Anne E. Phillips, Osie L. Byers; Los Angeles County General Hospital, Los Angeles, California: Clara Alice Henry.

1. 20 were assigned to the Tuskegee Army Air Field-Tuskegee, Alabama.
2. 30 were deployed to Liberia, Africa with the 256th Station Hospital
3. 15 were assigned to the 268th Station Hospital, the only medical unit staffed completely with Afro American personnel. The nurses arrived in Australia in November, 1943 and staged in Brisbane until the construction of the hospital was completed in Milne Bay, New Guinea in May, 1944. In May, 1945, the hospital was reassigned to Manila, Luzon, Philippine Island to support the impending invasion of Japan.
4. 16 nurses were in the China, Burma, India theater supporting the troops building the Burma and Ledo roads. Two units were subsequently formed: the 383rd Station Hospital and the 25th Station Hospital.
5. 20 nurses were on the staff of the Army Hospital in Warrington, England.

Within the U.S., nurses were also assigned to locations holding German and Italian prisoners of war, Japanese and Korean POWs were also cared for at:

Camp Beal, CA
Albuqerque, NM
San Luis Obsipo, CA
Fitzsimons Gen. Hosp., Denver, Co
Florence, AZ
Fort McCoy, WI
Ogden, UT
Rupert, ID

Many student nurses throughout the United States became Cadet Nurses. The Black nurses could not nurse White soldiers. The BLOOD was labeled "A." The Red Cross Pin had "A" under the number on the back.

Many army nurses cooperated therefore boards of pictures and videos were made. The boards of the army nurses were placed on display in Hawaii by General Colin Powell at one of the army conventions. After the convention, General Powell had the boards of pictures sent to the Defense Department in Washington in order to be accessible to anyone desiring their use in displays.

Various universities, departments and authors made contact with Hathaway. She made a roster of the nurses who cooperated and sent the pictures and roster. The authors recorded the nurses' responses. The universities invited Hathaway to speak at their schools. Various schools' "Career Day" programs have had her speak with her display of the pictures. The Mary Mahonny Club had a "Salute" program to the WW II Army nurses who live in Detroit. For Veterans Day observance many churches had Hathaway as a speaker with the pictures on display.

1980s: In order to enlighten the world (now ten years ago) Hathaway contacted the Oprah Winfrey Show for an audience with those army nurses who would cooperate. She would not interview. One of Hathaway's co-workers (a white teacher in Tacoma, Washington, wrote and asked Oprah if she would interview the African American nurses of World War II). The response was: "Thanks for your letter." and no followup. Hathaway contacted the editor of EBONY magazine and the answer was that he would think about it. Two years later, she wrote and asked if he had finished thinking. No response. The CRISIS editor of the NAACP was asked to do an article and his response was that he did not need such an article. No more contributions after years of donations. Hathaway sent a video of the nurses to Montel Williams to be shown on his TV program. Never a response from him!

Many army museums and veterans' hospitals have received the boards of pictures. They may be viewed in Bethune Museum in Washington, D.C., and in the Michigan Women's Historical Center and Hall of Fame in Lansing, Michigan. The African American Museum in Detroit was contacted over five years ago with a curator who looked at the pictures and would not accept them. From that time to the present, phone calls have been made to the Director and Curator; messages were left on their recording phone; no response. The Director, on one phone call, stated she would give Hathaway a return call; no call to date. The only response to all of the negative reactions is to send the material to the Historical Museum in Washington, D.C.

Several TV stations have interviewed Hathaway with a couple of army nurses. In the beginning of this project, channel 62 interviewed Hathaway and Polly Lathon Rawls; later the Eta Phi Beta Sorority editor Nina Mack Lester on channel 62 interviewed Hathaway and Rose Robinson. A southern Illinois news reporter from Puducah, Kentucky at the request of Hathaway's niece, Kelly, a freshman in high school, came to the school to interview her. As Hathaway spoke to the students, he produced the session on the evening TV News Report.

During this period of enlightenment, Hathaway's husband began having severe respiratory problems. He was placed on oxygen constantly and within a year developed emphysema. LH would not stop smoking and on February 1, 1993 he died. After forty years of marriage, it took time to adjust to changes in one's life. Her project filled the void.

The University in San Marcus, Texas; Army Historical Conference Washington D.C., WW II National Commemorative Association, Inc. in Indianapolis, Indiana, all had Hathaway to speak on the topic: "African American WW II Army Nurses." The Article in the WW II National Commemorative Association, Inc. was the beginning of many organizations that had Hathaway as their speaker. It was in Indianapolis that the program was shared with Brigadier General Wilma L. Vaught, U.S. Air Force Retired, President, Women's Military Service Memorial Foundation, Inc. Women In Military Service For America Memorial at Arlington National Cemetery. (The Memorial was completed Oct. 1997.)

Ted Talbert (channel 4), a friend of the family, heard about Hathaway's possessions of the WW II Army nurses' pictures. He made contact, and had her interviewed for a video entitled "Black Angels of Mercy" and had it narrated on Channel 4 by Emery King, reporter. Retired Lieutenant Colonel John Cannan in Seattle, Washington, obtained permission to use the video when he interviewed army nurse Ollie Hall, who served in Warrington, England, with Mary L. Petty, chief nurse. They could only nurse prisoners of war, no white American soldiers.

Judith Booker of C.W.D. Design came to Hathaway's home to pick up a chair that needed upholstering. When she saw the boards of pictures of the African American WW II army nurses she became interested in their being shown throughout America. Immediately she made contact with a friend in New York who knew the Congressional Black Caucus President, Congressman Charles Rangel. During their WW II Commemoration session, Prudence (Hathaway) Burns Burrell was invited to speak and to receive a "Certification of Appreciation for her contribution during World War II" from President William Clinton and Congressman Charles Rangel. Mayor Dennis Archer of Detroit attended the reception and had pictures taken with him and his wife, and army nurse Octavia Tillman Card. Having received such an outstanding award, she was interviewed and the contents of this interview were shown on TV channel 2 by Huel Perkins, anchor man.

During her Washington visit and speech in the program, Prudence Burrell met Ron JE. Armstead MCP., L.S.W. Executive Coordinator Congressional Black Caucus, Veterans Braintrust, Washington, D.C., Veterans Clearing House Inc. Boston, Massachusetts. He kept in touch and asked Prudence to speak at the Illinois State University, Bloomington, Illinois Black Social Workers Conference featuring African American veterans. They also gave a ticket to the program with Maya Angelo as guest speaker.

In the midst of Hathaway continuing with her project of publicity for the army nurses of World War II, she received a telephone call. Tragedy!! Hathaway's mentor who had helped her most of her life had suffered instant death. Hathaway went to the mentor's home and spent many months with her sister. Today there is constant contact with the sister and other family members.

Hathaway project continues yearly with Tuskegee Airmen's Week of Veterans' displays, African Americans programs, the 761st Tank Battalion & Allied Veterans, speeches in churches, veterans' programs, the 2nd Baptist Church in 1996 gave a beautiful award. These and many speeches during Career Days in elementary and secondary schools. Students in secondary schools are greeted in four different languages and the children are thrilled to respond. They are told that each one of them is born with a potential; to follow it up and they can stand tall, be independent and receive respect wherever they go because they can contribute to society. Kindergarten, first and second grade students are shown pictures of their age group from Australia, New Guinea, and Philippines; pictures of animals from the various countries. During the session, they are taught how to feel their pulse beat.

From the cooperation of many African American WW II army nurses sending in pictures in uniforms, Hathaway as commentator has made a video. These are circulating throughout the United States. The video ends with an outstanding vocalist, Mr. Norman Thrasher, singing "Never Look Back–No Matter What Was Your Misfortune."

HaHa.

THANKS......May God Bless!

The Authors who have made contact with Hathaway (Prudence Burns Burrell) for articles to be included in their books are:

GI Nightengales: Army Nurses Corp in WW II, Barbara B. Tomblin, 16 North Gates Rd., Mendham, NJ 07945

No Time for Fear, Diane Fessler, 5738 N. Central Ave., Phoenix, Arizona 85012-1316

We're in This War Too, Judy Barrett Litoff and Dacid Smith, Oxford University Press, 2001 Evans Road, Cary, NC 27513

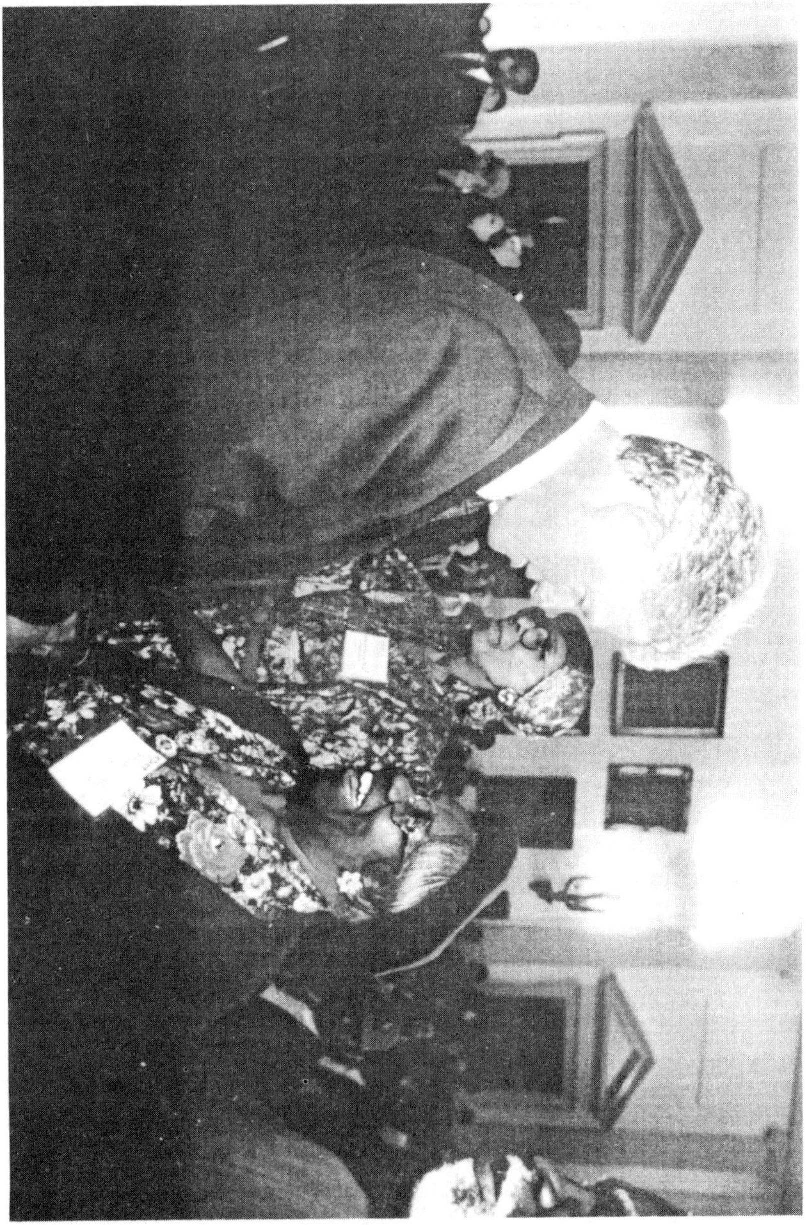

Lt. Prudence Burnes and Lt. Mayers in Sydney, Australia, 1943

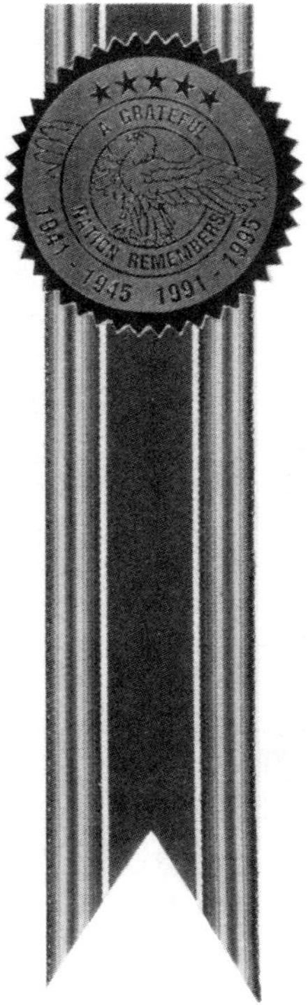

President of the United States,
World War II Commemoration Committee
and the Congressional Black Caucus

CERTIFICATE OF APPRECIATION

is Awarded to

1st Lieutenant
Prudence Burns Burrell

A Grateful Nation Remembers Your Sacrifices and Contributions During World War II

Claude M. Kicklighter

Charles B. Rangel

William J. Clinton

Opera House, Sydney, Australia

Dress required after 6:00 p.m. to ward off malaria carrying anopheles mosquitoes

268 Station Hospital stationed in the South Pacific—1945 joined Gen. McArthur in Manila for invasion into Japan.

1st Black graduate from University of Minnesota School of Public Health.

Riding the camel in Egypt.

Australian children.

Holding a koala in Australia.

Kangaroos in Brisbane, Australia

Feeding birds in Australia.

Thursday Island young boys danced at the World's Fair in Australia.

New Guinea Natives.

New Guinea Native Children.

1961—Prudence (Hathaway) Burns started the "Paramedics Club" in San Francisco, which replaced the "Future Nurse Club."

Gen. Wilma Vaught and Prudence Burns Burrell, speakers in Indianapolis, 1994.

Women's Historical Center in Lansing, MI.

Women's Historical Society Director, Gladys Beckwith in front of photos of Black Army Nurses in World War II.